Retro Salida

Retro Salida:

Short Histories from the Archive

Joy Jackson

Range Press
Salida, Colorado
2021

ISBN: 978-0-578-67721-7

Cover image: *Rocky Mountain Views on the Rio Grande, "The Scenic Line of the World": consisting of Twenty-Three Colored Views from Recent Photographs. Made exclusively for the Van Noy Inter-State Company, Denver, Colorado. For sale only en route on the Denver & Rio Grande Western Railroad.* Engraved, printed, and published by the Smith-Brooks Printing Company, Denver, Colorado, U.S.A., 1917.

Frontispiece: *A Bird's Eye View of Salida ca. 1888.* Dick Dixon Collection, part of the Salida Centennial Photo Archive, Salida Regional Library.

For Damon

On June 24, [1880] the name of the town was changed from the awkward and unmusical 'South Arkansas' to the beautiful, euphonious, and expressive 'Salida.' The editor rejoiced in the change, thanked Governor Hunt for his kindness, [was] told what the word meant, and impressed the people with the importance of giving it the proper pronunciation, 'Sah-lee-dah.'

I am sorry to record that his instructions have been woefully disregarded.

- Salida Mail, June 5, 1900

Table of Contents

A winter bird's eye view of Salida, taken ca. 1950s.
The Denver & Rio Grande's art deco depot, seen here at the end of
F Street, was built in 1941 and served as a dual railway-bus
passenger station. It was very chic and modern with stone
banding, flat roofs, angular outlines, and vertical towers. It was
razed in January 1985.

Retro Salida

Introduction

The roots of Salida begin in 1880, when the Denver & Rio Grande Railroad Company won the rights to build rail through Bighorn Sheep Canyon, then known as the Grand Canon of the Arkansas. Once they built through to the Arkansas Valley, the D&RG set up the new settlement town of Salida, named by Governor Hunt. Gov. Hunt was an incorporator of the D&RG, and along with agents Millie Ohmertz and William Van Every, was instrumental in the new town's founding. They were in essence, the 'money,' and built or helped fund many of the buildings in town.

These buildings were slap-dashed, wooden affairs which soon became eyesores. Several structure fires swept through town during that first decade, which resulted in the construction of beautiful new buildings, built with brick from the local brickworks. Many of these buildings still stand and as a result, Salida has the largest historic district in Colorado.

Salida was a raucous town for its first twenty years, filled with gunslingers and cattle thieves, whorehouses and bars. It was a difficult task for local law enforcement to keep the peace.

In these early days, Salida catered to the Denver & Rio Grande's employees: the firemen, engineers, agents, and mechanics. The town also took care of the miners who were newly come to Colorado in search of mineral wealth. The mountains around Monarch were producing gold and silver, lead-silver, zinc, and copper and the money the miners earned was spent in Salida. The local madams and saloons enjoyed a brisk business during this time.

By the early 20th century, the mineral wealth was dwindling. With the advent of the automobile, the Denver & Rio Grande Western Railroad began to dwindle as well.

The D&RGW ran its last passenger train in 1964, though freight trains continued to run through Salida to points west. Officially, the last train that went through Salida was in 1997, Union Pacific's engine 844. When Climax molybdenum mine in Leadville closed around the same time, the town of Salida became economically depressed.

But Salida and the surrounding area has always been a magnet for tourists. The healing hot spring waters and the meditative views of the Sawatch Range have always been a palliative to those in need of physical and mental comfort. With the advent of recreation tourism, the Arkansas River changed Salida's fate, and tourists brought in some much-needed revenue. Some stayed. People who loved the mountains and the river eventually turned Salida into a town with an active population and a rich historic past.

Today, Union Pacific owns the old Denver & Rio Grande lines that are still visible in Salida and in Bighorn Sheep Canyon. They are one of the last vestiges of the D&RG, along with the railroad's old shop building.

The Salida Archive is the Salida Regional Library's repository of the town's past. The online archive, as it is, was built by myself, and it has been updated in the past decade to include histories from the surrounding areas of Granite, Leadville, and the Monarch Mining

Region. The reader may supplement this book with more images and history available online at <u>salidalibrary.org</u>.

Beginning in March 2016, each chapter in this book appeared as an article in The Mountain Mail and each was inspired by something that was in the archive. The title *Retro Salida* comes from the Latin 'retro' meaning 'retrospectively' and the Spanish 'salida' meaning 'gateway.' More poetically it could be read as 'Portal Into the Past.'

Retro Salida came about as a side project in an effort to keep the entire document together. The chapters are updated and revised, along with necessary omissions, corrections, and enhancements. Any discrepancies herein are my own. — J.Jackson

One

The Ute People

According to the Ute Creation Story, the creator placed the Ute people in the Rocky Mountains. The Ute people have always been here, and will always be here.

One of the oldest places in this area that records the history of the indigenous peoples is up at the Monarch Game Drive, just north of Monarch Ski Area on the Continental Divide Trail. These game drives are over 5,000 years old and were used to herd deer and elk into low-walled enclosures where hunters would wait in ambush.

Over time, the indigenous peoples separated into bands. One of these bands was the Ute people, who lived peacefully with the land, migrating often to keep their footprint light on the earth and to let game herds replenish.

Foresters Fred Agee and Joseph Cuenin wrote *A History of the Cochetopa National Forest* in 1925 and they dedicated a chapter to the Ute people:

"Antelope, buffalo, deer, elk, mountain sheep, and other game were abundant in those days, and the region around Cochetopa Pass [in Saguache County] appears to have been a favorite hunting ground for the Utes. Trails worn down into the solid granite on Sawtooth Mountain by ages of travel bear mute testimony of the extensive use of that country by the Indians long before the advent of the white men. Their main trail from the eastern to the western slope crossed the Continental Divide over the present Cochetopa Pass."

The Ute people camped in our region as well, and used certain hilltops in the Arkansas Valley to create signal fires as a means of communication:

"The high ridge jutting into the Arkansas Valley near Brown's Creek and the tall butte near Shirley [close to O'Haver Lake] were favorite signaling points for the Utes. The arranging of rocks in certain ways by passing parties served the place of written communication in advising their friends which way they were traveling and how they were faring. Fires were also used in signaling when help was urgently needed."

Besides hunting and traveling in what is now most of Colorado, battles between the different tribes were a common occurrence. Counting coup was an integral part of a young man's ability to prove his courage and attain a higher ranking in the tribe. There were skirmishes aplenty:

"The Utes were a powerful tribe of Indians and in the early wars easily held their own against the fierce Arapahoes on the east and the savage Cheyennes of the north, whether fighting in their mountain fastness or on the open plains. The rocks just west of Villa Grove and the old battle field on Ute Pass near Saguache, where 126 graves may be counted, are grim reminders of the sanguinary conflicts between them."

Once the Spaniards introduced the horse in the 16th century, horse dealing and horse stealing became part of the scene. For the next 200 years, the Spaniards and Utes would engage in trading and eventually, hostilities. As the Spanish became increasingly aggressive, the Ute people would band together with other tribes and raid Spanish horse stock.

Mexico ceded what is now the southwestern U.S. in 1848 and in 1861, the Colorado territory was formed which opened the floodgates for white people to enter into Ute lands. It wasn't long before the Ute people learned that they were trading one Anglo enemy for another. Anglo ears were still ringing with the credo of Manifest Destiny and they were on a mission to either homogenize the Ute people, or to eliminate them.

With Chaffee County's mountainous landscape, the Utes were insofar lucky to be relatively isolated from incoming whites. It was a different story in California. During the Gold Rush, miners would engage in 'shooting parties' of Native Americans. Historian Hubert Howe Bancroft wrote about this state-sponsored genocide that occurred during the mid-19th century in California:

"The savages were in the way; the miners and settlers were arrogant and impatient; there were no missionaries or others present with even the poor pretense of soul-saving or civilizing. It was one of the last human hunts of civilization, and the basest and most brutal of them all...Sufficient excuse was offered for the miners and settlers to band and shoot down any Indians they met, old or young, innocent or guilty, friendly or hostile, until their appetite for blood was appeased."

Around the time of California's Gold Rush, there were ten Native Americans to a single white person. By the end of 1849, that number had dropped to two to one. Most of these Native Americans died due to massacre or the forced conditions of starvation and disease.

Here in Colorado, the recent Sand Creek Massacre in which hundreds of U.S. cavalrymen attacked and murdered over 200 Cheyenne & Arapaho people was fresh in everyone's minds. The Ute people were finding it harder and harder to live amongst the Anglos:

"The Indians claimed the settlers encroached upon their lands. The settlers accused the Indians of stealing their horses and cattle. Reprisals by the settlers were not infrequent."

In 1868, a treaty was formed between the U.S. Government and the Ute people. It designated as reservation land the western half of Colorado, pushing the Utes out of their original swath of territory. In 1873, the Brunot Agreement was enacted which took away nearly 4 million acres of the San Juans from the Southern Utes, making it available for mining to whites.

Through the years, skirmishes between Anglos and Utes occurred with more frequency. These histories are recorded elsewhere, but the two most notable were the killing of Chief Shavano's son with its subsequent reprisal, and then the White River uprising and the killing of Nathan Meeker. Every confrontation added to the mountain of animosity. Whites relentlessly perpetuated propaganda to push the Ute people out of Colorado. Triggered by all these occurrences, the Ute Bill was passed, which effectively took another 11 million acres from the Ute people. In 1880, this paragraph appeared in the Mountain Mail:

"The Ute Bill has finally become a law ... The bill as passed is far from satisfactory to the people of Colorado because they had hoped that the Utes would be removed from the State entirely. A great deal has been said to the effect that if the miners were permitted to go in unmolested they would soon settle the Ute question."

Colorado was one step away from Ute genocide. Eventually, it was assimilate or die, and the Ute people had no choice but to accept their relocation to reservations to escape complete annihilation.

Forty years after the dispossession of the Utes took place, Agee & Cuenin wrote this of the Ute people:

"Notwithstanding sporadic outbreaks, the Ute confederacy was never at open warfare with the whites, nor was the tribe as a whole ever hostile to the numerous parties of immigrants coming to or passing through the country during the two decades following the acquisition of the territory from Mexico."

Because their touch on the land was so light, there is just a hint of where the Ute people lived and thrived. Archaeologists have recently discovered remnants of wikiups on Colorado forest land. These were the wood structures that the ancestral Utes used in setting up their lodges. Like the Utes, they have withstood time, and destruction.

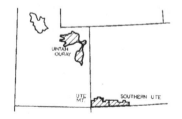

Current map of Ute reservations in Colorado and Utah.

Two

Hidden Treasure of the Spaniards

I n the 1600s, Spanish explorers had roamed into the territory that is now Colorado. Major expeditions were documented, minor ones were not. During this time, a legend was born in Chaffee County: Spaniards buried a treasure of gold near Mt. Princeton, then drew up a map on animal hide which recorded the location. After a skirmish with the Utes, the Spaniards died, leaving a fortune waiting to be found.

Spanish exploration was still occurring into the 1870s, with the Rivera and Escalante expeditions both traversing through southwest Colorado. Legend has it that an undocumented expedition from Mexico made it into the upper Arkansas Valley. Once there, the group secretly mined a fortune in gold near Mt. Princeton. Unbeknownst to them, they were being tracked by Utes. The tale is as follows:

"Below where Buena Vista now stands, Chalk Creek comes down from Alpine pass to flow into the Arkansas at Nathrop. Just down the river is a beautiful valley coming in from the west. It is really the Chalk Creek valley, separated from the stream by a long parallel swell of ground. At the lower end, on the eastern side, the travelers [i.e. Spaniards] camped for the night. The place is visible from the Denver & Rio Grande trains just after the track climbs up out of Brown's Canon across the bridge over the Arkansas. There the level valley ends abruptly in a steep, rocky slope. Here the camp was made. The mules were picketed. The gold in sacks was piled close to the campfire. Two men with guns were stationed close by as a special precaution against any attack. The sun went down beyond the massive brow of Mount Princeton. The shadows deepened in the great gulches below. Night came to the valley — a night clear and silent as death. The men slumbered, all save the guard. Suddenly the silence was rent and shattered by the unutterable yell of the Indians. The red men seemed to come up out of the ground all around. Then followed a fierce battle."

Ute and Spaniard brutally killed one another. Then the remaining Utes fled, leaving just two Spaniards alive. These two immediately came up with a plan to hide their gold before the Utes returned. They dug a hole and, using the skin of one of their dead mules, they wrapped the gold within and buried it: "It was a gruesome task. The night was still. The dead lay all about them. At any moment they might hear the yell of the red men or the crack of a gun." The Spaniards then drew a map, presumably on mule skin, with details outlining the location of buried treasure. They escaped back to Mexico but died soon after. The map and the tale of the hidden treasure was left behind and it soon became legend to the folks of Chaffee County:

"There is a man in Salida who knows an old timer who is acquainted with the brother of one of the men who buried the gold, and has seen the chart many times. By its aid, parties have many times tried to dig up the fortune … Many people have dug in vain. The gold is unquestionably there, but it has been hard to locate it."

In 1913, half-mad miner Thomas Summers came out of the hills of Nathrop and into Salida to remind everyone of the hidden treasure buried on the mountain's doorstep. And this is when the tale really began to flourish. A miner for over thirty years, Summers believed the treasure was buried inside of Mt. Princeton. He had been searching for a few years but was at a standstill because he didn't own the land he was attempting to dig on, so he came into Salida with the express purpose of gaining partners and acquiring cash to purchase deeds to the land. Summers had proof, of a sort: maps and a detailed handbook that he wrote in to keep track of all of the history related to the treasure:

"There is something about his conversation that is almost convincing, for when he talks, he leans far over and looks his audience squarely in the eyes, and usually during this time, he is tracing over the lines of some illegible drawings in a small, worn notebook, which he has available at all times. The drawings he did himself, and some he calls human faces, and some are human skulls, and others are drawings of animals which he declares are to be found carved in the face of the mountain — if only a person will hunt them out when the full moon shines from a certain angle overhead."

The embellishments added by Summers made the legend a fully realized story now. He believed that hidden inside of Mt. Princeton, long and meandering tunnels held vast treasures, "guarded by human skulls, and strange, weird figures of stone … resting, undisturbed, through the past hundred or more years."

And some of his charts, which were written in Spanish, read: "Measurement is taken from the face of the Spanish princess, which is a face in the mountain, resembling the countenance of the beautiful royal highness."

After igniting a storm of curiosity in Salida, Summers headed back to his small cabin near Mt. Princeton, "where he will attempt to brave the winter snows while he searches for the buried horde." He had found no associates to assist him in his task.

In 1937, a map, possibly drawn up by Thomas Summers or maybe even the two Spaniards, was printed in the local paper showing the location of the hidden treasure of the Spaniards. It included a paragraph (written in Spanish) with instructions to the location:

"En un valle redondo como una manzana uno cruz fornlada por d[e] Rio y dos arroyos, mirando para arriba el Rio seguir el arroyo a mano izquirda 1/4 de una milla hasta ilegar a un lago pegueno-hacia agua blanca entre el lago y el rio astan quatro. arboles formando va cuadro, tres vocas an aiferentos puntos, una marcada con el signo de manos brochados y otra con una cruz."

and translated here:

"In a rounded valley like an apple, a cross is formed by a river and two washes. Looking upriver, follow the left wash 3/4 of a mile to arrive at a small lake, to white water between the lake and the river. There are four trees forming a square. There are three rocks in different points, one marked with the sign of clasped hands and the other with a cross."

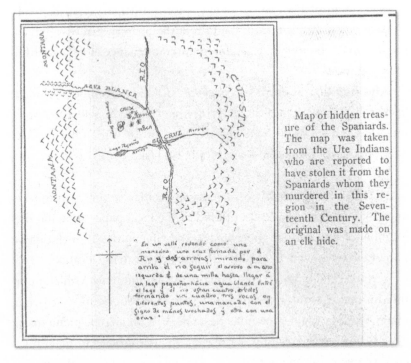

Map of hidden treasure of the Spaniards. The map was taken from the Ute Indians who are reported to have stolen it from the Spaniards whom they murdered in this region in the Seventeenth Century. The original was made on an elk hide.

Whether Thomas Summers or some other lucky miner actually found the treasure is unknown. It is rumored that there are still several other hidden Spanish caches buried in the county.

Three

The Denver & Rio Grande Company

T he economic and opportunistic ambition that defined the
westward expansion led to miners and other settlers entering
Colorado to exploit the natural resources. Railroad corporations,
determined to satisfy the demand of these adventurers, laid rails
west. One of these, the Denver & Rio Grande Company, was
incorporated in October 1870 and was named for two points on the
future railroad line. Their plan was to build a trunk line from Denver
to Mexico City, and then have branches extend west from that line.
The main line would start from Denver and travel down the Rio
Grande River, the headwaters of which start here in central Colorado.

Historian Arthur Ridgway wrote the following lines about the
newness of the land and the untapped resources that were waiting:

"The [D&RG's] articles of incorporation very succinctly
emphasize the fact that the country to the west of the main trunk line
was even then virtually unknown and unexplored. The descriptions
of such branch lines as were included in the original incorporation
articles were very general indeed, and leave a correct impression that
the whole country to the west was veiled in an atmosphere of
mystery. Practically the entire territory to be traversed by the

proposed line was public domain. Right of way could not be purchased, neither were there any federal statutes by which a right of way could be confirmed to a railroad. As a result of the efforts of the original promoters [i.e. D&RG] a special law was enacted by the National Congress on June 15, 1872, confirming to the Denver and Rio Grande the right of way 200 feet wide in public domain."

In 1871, the Denver & Rio Grande built their first line from Denver to Colorado City (now Colorado Springs). By 1872, the rails had been laid to Pueblo and Florence, but stopped short of Canon City due to a dispute with rival railroad company the Atchison, Topeka, & Santa Fe.

Though the courts may have given legal right to the D&RG to build rail, this new law didn't sit well with the AT&SF. Therein began a battle as to who would lay rails through the Grand Canon of the Arkansas, which is today Bighorn Sheep Canyon.

Local jurisdiction sided with the Santa Fe railway, due to the D&RG's questionable business tactics, one of which was setting up company-owned town sites and bypassing existing town sites, essentially snuffing out their existence.

In 1878, the Santa Fe crew fought back and with a local force of men seized the road into the Canon. Gordon Chappell describes the hostilities:

"Most of the battle was fought out in the courts, clear up to that final arbiter, the United States Supreme Court, whose decision in this case, however, failed to settle the matter. At lower levels, both railroads had judges prejudiced in their favor ... The war did involve some violence; both sides hired gunfighters such as the Santa Fe's William Barclay 'Bat' Masterson, and twenty miles west of Canon City, the Rio Grande forces constructed rock entrenchments such as 'Fort DeRemer' to prevent the Santa Fe people from building west of the gorge."

The court battle was officially over in March of 1880 when both sides signed a compromise agreement: generally speaking, AT&SF would not build rail into the Sawatch and Sangre de Cristo mountain ranges heading west and D&RG would not build eastward into the plains.

The race was now on to build rail to Leadville and other points situated near new mining prospects. The Denver & Rio Grande tracklayers began laying rail through the Grand Canon of the Arkansas. Arthur Ridgway estimated during this time that there

were no less than 500 surveyors in "every practicable canon and pass in the mountains south and west of Denver."

By May 1, 1880 the tracklayers had reached the D&RG settlement town of South Arkansas (now Salida). As a matter of course, the AT&SF settlement of Cleora, 2 miles east, was bypassed. The tracklayers pushed on and Nathrop had rails by the first of June. Leadville was glittering in the distance.

About 600 people populated Cleora (currently where Rocky Mountain Livestock's Sale Barn is) in 1880. Once the D&RG came through, they sensed the imminent death of their town and picked up everything they owned, buildings included, to settle in the new town of South Arkansas.

At South Arkansas, the D&RG was making money selling off plats of land that first year:

"The Denver and Rio Grande Company owned all of the South Arkansas town site a short time ago. But it is not so now. They have sold the greater portion of the lots to people who have come and are

The Denver & Rio Grande Roundhouse with shops in the rear. Tenderfoot Mountain is visible to the right.

still coming, and on these lots business houses and residences are going up at a rapid rate."

Territorial Governor and D&RG civil engineer Alexander Hunt was a founding father of the new town, and he and his wife soon rechristened it Salida, Spanish for 'exit' or 'gateway.' By 1886, the

D&RG employed 250 people in Salida and the roundhouse held 42 locomotives. The new town had become the hub for six major branch lines of the railroad.

But by 1892, the relationship was souring. Animosity was fomenting between Salida and the railroad. What happened? Salida was by then a destination town; perhaps the influx of tourists and health seekers that the trains were bringing in was wearing thin on Salidans. In April of that year, Mayor Wright chided townsfolk:

"Some people look on that corporation [i.e. the D&RG] as a great vulture hovering over a dead carcass. This is an erroneous idea and our people should disabuse their minds of any such delusions. It is the presence of the Rio Grande that gives to our homes a large part of their value. We have hardly a citizen that does not draw either directly or indirectly a subsistence from that corporation."

Salida was naturally separated from the railroad by the Arkansas River, which may have contributed to an 'Us vs. Them' attitude. But then as now, tourism was Salida's bread and butter, and the railroad brought in a lot of tourists. The railroad was also a major employer of many Salidans. In the end, money brought in by the railroad settled the niceties, and they learned to get along with each other.

The railroad's expansion west was a momentous undertaking and the D&RG will always be the reason why the town of Salida is here:

"It was not until 1880, when that little giant of the West, the Denver & Rio Grande Railroad, succeeded in drilling and blasting its way through the now world-famous Royal Gorge, along the course of the Arkansas River, that access to the valley from the east was possible. It was for a long time thought impracticable to cut a railroad line through this stupendous piece of solid rock over seven miles in length. Granite ledges were here extending their massive peaks thousands of feet in the air, and seemingly only leaving room for the swift, rushing Arkansas to roar on its mad course to the Mississippi. In time though, after months of perseverance and the expenditure of millions of dollars the Salida (Exit) was made, and behold, before them lay thousands of acres of beautiful, fertile land, liberally favored by Nature both in the matter of its immediate situation and surroundings."

Four

A Founding Family of Salida

F red Bateman was one of the first kids to live in Salida. His dad, George, was a tinsmith by trade and tinsmiths were in high demand here in Chaffee County in the 19th century. The miners and railroaders who were migrating through needed light, durable cookware, and it needed to be easily repaired if it got damaged.

The Batemans were originally from Illinois but patriarch George suffered from such debilitating asthma that he sold all of his possessions, with the exception of his 'tinner's tools,' and moved his young family out to Colorado to alleviate his symptoms.

The Batemans landed in Pueblo in 1873 where George worked in a hardware store while his wife tended to the kids. When George's wife died in 1879, the two youngest kids, Walter and Mable, were sent back to Illinois to live with their aunt. Teen-aged Fred stayed on with his dad and he remembered these days in an interview with Richard Carroll, about 40 years later: "Father and I moved into a little place where we 'bached.' Upon me fell the cooking and household work, and a 13 year-old boy is not very proficient. But I remember roasting a turkey that year for Thanksgiving."

His dad soon felt the bug to go into business for himself amid news that the Denver & Rio Grande Railroad was laying rails west. In January 1880, George and Fred followed the railroaders into Canon City and beyond. Fred remembered the trip up from Canon City to Cleora:

"I went from Pueblo with the freighter who hauled my father's tools and a small stock of goods. It took eight days to make the trip for the load was heavy. There were many freight teams on the road, causing many delays at narrow places. We came through Canon City, [then] Grape Creek to Vallie, and then to Cleora. The railroad had not reached Vallie [just southeast of Howard] yet. We crossed the site of Salida at a point on present F Street, about 60 feet northeast of 2nd Street; but not a house was in sight from there, and Salida was unheard of."

George and his son ended up in Buena Vista. Many towns can claim to have been the 'Wickedest City in the West' but Fred points the finger at Buena Vista:

"Poncha Springs, Maysville, Garfield, and St. Elmo were sizable towns but Buena Vista was the largest town. It was the end of the Denver, South Park, and Pacific Railroad, afterwards the Colorado Southern. Most all of the merchandise, supplies and passengers for Leadville, which was booming, came over this little narrow gauge railroad. Nineteen to twenty large stage coaches fully loaded left Buena Vista every morning and returned every night. Hundreds of freight teams were on the road. One outfit, the Dickey Brothers, were said to have over 100 six-mule teams. Buena Vista was a booming town with all sorts of edifices, from a simple tent to a respectable business building. As we went in, we passed a saloon in a big tent with a board front and a huge sign proclaiming, 'The Mule Skinners Retreat.' There were four dance halls and a score of saloons, most of them with open gambling, roulette, faro bank, and stud poker ... A feud grew up between the mule skinners and the townspeople and many killings resulted. It is the writer's opinion that in all the West there was not a tougher town than Buena Vista in 1880."

Perhaps the lawlessness of Buena Vista is what decided George to take his son out of there. The Denver & Rio Grande Railroad was moving in from Canon City and had begun building the town of Salida. George opened Bateman's Hardware Store in Salida in May 1880, one of the first businesses to lay down a foundation here. Fred remembers:

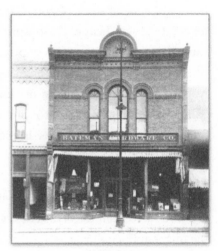

119 F Street

"We heard that a new town was to start near Cleora which was to be a division point for the Denver & Rio Grande Railroad, so my father went down to investigate it. In May of 1880, we moved to Salida, then called South Arkansas ... This newly-born town was then the end of the rails of the Denver & Rio Grande. The town was just building and houses were being moved up from Cleora; but tents and canvas-roofed shacks were in the majority. Father rented a plot of ground, on west 1st Street near G, from Peter Mulvany, and there

built a shack about 20 by 30 feet:
then he started a tin shop and
store. I worked with him,
excepting the two winters I spent
in school at Pueblo. We were
rather poor, so I had to work for
my board and room while going
to school. I earned some money
during the summer months selling
papers on the streets; and trout,
which I caught in the South
Arkansas River, so I managed to
get along."

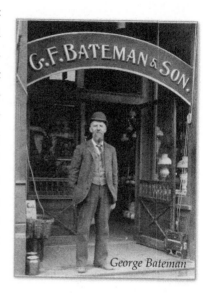

George Bateman

George Bateman eventually became one of the first incorporators
of the town of Salida and was one of the town's first councilmen. He
relocated his business to 119 F Street. Fred remembers:

"When the railroad started building over Marshall Pass many
people left Salida, and the town didn't grow much for several years,
but we got along and gradually made a business. In 1887, I became of
age [at 21] and my father gave me a third interest in the business. The
name was changed to G.F. Bateman & Son."

By this time, the youngest son Walter was back with the family
and when he turned 21, George gave him the final third in Bateman's
Hardware Company. Besides having their tin shop on site, the
Batemans kept Salida supplied with stoves, ranges, sporting goods
(including bicycles), and mining supplies. Walter Bateman did house
calls for customers who needed plumbing and heating work.

Interior of Bateman Hardware

The Batemans were a cornerstone family of Salida, cementing their status when Fred and Walter helped organize Salida's first bicycle club in 1894.

Five

A Trip to Gothic

In the spring of 1879, wire silver (naturally occurring strands of silver) was discovered in the Sylvanite Mine, just north of Crested Butte. News quickly broke out in all the Colorado papers. A correspondent for the Saguache Chronicle reported in July 1879:

"There is at present quite an excitement here over the discovery of a vein of wire silver in Gothic Mountain. I saw a specimen of ore which appears to be almost pure silver; certainly safe to say 50% silver. The vein of wire silver is reported to be 13 inches thick, besides which there is a thickness of 3 feet of ore which assays to show to contain 1,000 oz. of silver to the ton. As a natural consequence, there is a general rush to that locality. A town has been laid out to which is given the name of Gothic City."

That was all it took. That summer, thousands of people poured into the Gunnison country. One local reported seeing in a single day over 250 horse-drawn teams on the road to Gunnison and Gothic.

The following summer, on May 5, 1880, Rachel Bradbury left Canon City with her husband Charles, his parents, and his brothers along with their wives. They were en route to Gothic in search of 'silver wires.' Rachel kept a diary of their summer trip.

The trip itinerary took them through the Grand Canon of the Arkansas and down into the San Luis Valley before heading up to Gothic. Ten days into the trip, Rachel and her family were encamped near Del Norte, visiting with friends. This, from Rachel's diary:

"Monday morning, May 17th. We are still visiting and my program is washing today. Now two of our men have gone to Alamosa, that is 35 miles down the river and the rest of our numbers are still in camp. Afternoon is very windy and I have just had a race after a piller that was put out to air."

About 3 weeks into their journey, the group was still in the San Luis Valley. Illness began to plague the travelers. Here is Rachel's entry for May 30:

"[It's] just after breakfast of coffee, biscuit, butter, hominy, syrup, breakfast bacon. Let me see what the ailments [are] in this tent. Two have sore throats and one of them is in bed. Another has a boil on his neck and a fourth has a sore eye so that leaves but one that has no ailments and she is out climbing mountains. There are thirteen of us traveling together and [we] have three teams. Some of our fellow travelers have been spending their time fishing today. They caught 26 trout in all."

The next day the group was climbing Cochetopa Pass heading towards Gunnison:

"We have had some rough road to travel over this morning. After going about 8 miles, we stopped for dinner by the road side and made our tea as usual by a camp fire. We were traveling up the east side of the Cotchtop Pass this morning and are now about 1 ½ miles from the top. This pass is over the Grand Rocky Mountain Range.

There is an abundance of timber on each side of the road. It is quakenasp and pine timber ... The men had to double team to get up the top of the pass ... When we got about a mile down, the road was so sideling, the men had to tie ropes over the top of the wagons and hold on to keep them from going over. Also, they had to repair the road some so we were detained some time, till we got quite chilly. Our afternoon drive was short and very tiresome. All were very tired when we arrived in camp and some [were] very sick."

Illness was a constant presence during the 5-week journey to Gothic. Rachel only reports minor ailments, but due to the lack of clean water, it can be presumed that some of the travelers were sick with giardia. Some were also plagued by respiratory ailments.

A couple of days later Rachel and her family were heading north to Gothic:

"Now we are going toward the snow-capped Crestie Butte Mountains. Noon by the road, eat a cold dinner, rest a while and go on till we come to a mud hole and hill, where the men have to double team again and we get safely over and travel on to Brush Creek. There the water was up to the wagon wheels and current so swift the men fastened a rope to the end of each wagon tongue and nine men across the river held and pulled to keep the horses from being washed down the stream."

On June 10th, the group finally reached their summer encampment near Rock Creek at Gothic. During their stay, the men and boys tried their luck at finding some wire silver while Rachel and the other women stayed busy with homemaking, camp style. Unfortunately, many in the group were ill from their journey.

On Friday, June 12th, Rachel writes: "The weather is cool and beautiful. The program is ironing and baking. Four of us have severe colds and my voice is gone." A week later Rachel writes: "Our colds are like faithful friends." Charles' mother is the most severely ill. That night, not a week after they arrive in Gothic, 62-year-old Julia Bradbury passes away. Rachel writes:

"Death is in our midst and claims one of our numbers. A dear mother is called to pass from time to eternity. It is the Lord's will be done, not ours."

Time passes at camp and the acuteness of sorrow lessens. Spirits were cheerier by the end of the month:

"I baked [bread] for the men to take prospecting. By ten minutes after 10 o'clock, they were traveling to the mountains. I passed the time by reading, sleeping, and mending and the three children played pack horses and go a-prospecting. This has been a pleasant day."

And for the 4th of July, something special:

"We have ice cream to eat that is froze with snow and it was splendid. Also, we had a nice cake to eat with it. The milk was 15¢ a quart and eggs at the sale of 50¢ a dozen. In the evening, six of us take a walk up the mountains, picked some wildflowers, and I also had a horseback ride."

Gothic was a bustling town by this point. There were around 1,000 people living in Gothic in 1880 and many thousands more in the surrounding Gunnison countryside.

The summer eases on. Rachel spends her days taking care of camp, and writing in her diary. On Saturday, July 10th, she writes:

"We got up late this morning. Also, one of the men came in from Galena Mountain. All are well. We had several showers of rain today. This evening I sat down to write. My attention is called outside to look at a beautiful rainbow, the radiant colors arching down the side of the mountain. My work today is not worthy of note."

Excitement was brewing during this Colorado summer: Former President Ulysses Grant was coming to visit the state and planned to make stops at the mining towns in central Colorado. He began his journey in Salida with Governor John Routt. Biographer Albert Sandford wrote of the trip: "They started from Salida in a spring wagon drawn by a team of mountain ponies. They were out two weeks, camping along the way or stopping at some ranch house overnight, just as circumstances for their convenience and comfort suggested."

The route from Salida went over Poncha Pass and down towards the San Luis Valley, then west over Cochetopa Pass. When the party reached nearly to the top of Poncha Pass, they stopped for lunch:

"...They drew up beside an abandoned cabin. While Routt filled a water bucket from a stream, Grant took out his pocket knife and whittled two sets of knives and forks. The people at Salida who had packed the lunch had neglected to include silverware. While they ate, Grant inquired about the local history, asked the names of the mountains, watched some chipmunks, and fed crumbs from his lunch to a hungry camp robber. While reclining on the grass afterwards, he described this as one of the happiest days of his life."

On August 5, 1880, Grant stopped in Gothic and was welcomed by 50 mounted horseback riders, and then taken on a fishing expedition at Ohio Creek. A reception was held that evening at the Gothic Hotel. The whole town attended except for Rachel and her family since they were packing to leave the next morning but she writes that "the people of Gothic City felt highly honored by the arrival of General Grant."

Rachel and her family headed back to Canon City the next day and she never relates in her diary whether or not their endeavors in the mines at Gothic were successful. Eventually, the thin veins of wire silver proved to be too difficult to extract from the mountains so by 1881 the silver boom in Gothic had gone bust.

Six

Salida's Fire Boys

One of the first things a new town needs is a fire department and in 1880, the Salida Hose Company No. 1 was established. In January 1881, meetings were held and officers were elected. By-laws were soon drawn up. Then a call was put out: "All those who take an interest in this organization (and who does not) can now become members by signing these by-laws."

During these formative years, money was tight and City Council was not offering anything from their coffers, so Salida Hose Company No. 1 threw grand balls to raise money for their department. The first of these events, held in February of 1882, was described as "one of the finest entertainments ever attended by the people of this town … If any person left the ballroom without having danced as often as he desired it was his own fault. To show that there was a good crowd in attendance and that there was plenty of room, it is only necessary to remark that there were nine Virginia reels on the floor at once." That first ball brought into the fire department's treasury close to $75.

By September of 1882, Hose Company No. 1 was making requests to City Council for hose carts, hooks, chains, and ropes. The firefighters were not wearing any sort of protective gear at this time but they were busy working fires: that November, Bissell's Grocery, at 101 F, caught fire:

"The fire boys were prompt to respond and in an incredibly short space of time, two streams were turned onto the fire." It was a mystery how the blaze started but the editors at the Mountain Mail

newspaper commended the department: "Boys, you have the thanks and gratitude of every person in town, and more especially of those living in the same block in which the fire occurred."

By January 1883, the Company had a new hose house located at 114 E. 1st Street. It is described here:

"The convenient and practical arrangement of the house was the theme of universal comment. The bell tower is utilized by a large wooden drum, suspended near the summit underneath the place destined for the bell, on which the hose can be readily and expeditiously hoisted for the purpose of cleaning and drying, The hose, of which there is a sufficient length for all practical purposes on hand [about a 1000 feet], is linen, and can stand the big pressure that it sometimes has to stand, ... The larger portion of the hose house is, of course, occupied by the truck room. On the sides are conveniently arranged a number of leather buckets and a large supply of ladders of various lengths; a room in the rear is fitted up with a number of bunks for sleeping purposes ... After last night's meeting, the boys went out for an hour's practice with their apparatus. It worked like a charm. The water plugs showed an excellent pressure, and streams were thrown that went way above the tallest buildings—nay even above the big flagstaff. Our citizens may be rest assured that no fire that may break out in Salida within reach of its water-system, can get much of a start."

On New Year's Day, the 'gallant boys of Salida Hose Co. No. 1' celebrated by throwing a parade. Afterwards, a ball was held at the opera house to raise money to buy a bell for the tower at the hose house: "The terpsichorean exercises continued until three o'clock in the morning, when the assembly broke up in the greatest good humor, and the occasion was generally voted to be one of the most pleasant that Salida has seen since its foundation."

It appears they made their purchase of a bell because a few weeks later, A.T. Ryan's livery near the railroad tracks on W. 1st Street broke out in flames. That January morning, engine whistles from the Denver & Rio Grande Roundhouse and pistol shots from the local police sounded the alarm. Unfortunately, "the little fire bell in the hose tower did its best to add to the clangor but it was found to be entirely too small."

Several of the fire boys had been at a Knights of Pythias meeting when the fire began; with no time to change clothes, they fought the blaze in their Pythias uniforms. The Hose Company set to work on the fire but came across difficulties when it was discovered that the distance to the nearest fireplug was 800 feet. The friction caused by that distance eradicated most of the water pressure. Temperatures were below freezing and there was a blustery breeze blowing, adding to the wind chill: "Some of the fire boys had their noses, ears, and fingers seriously injured by the intense cold ... J.M. Buster stuck to the nozzle 'til he was covered with ice from head to foot, and he had to be taken by his friends to be resuscitated. Charlie Rose didn't care for himself when it came to saving property and was completely broken up by his superhuman exertions."

A.T. Ryan's livery was a complete loss; six horses were killed. The fact that he had no insurance made the loss more heartbreaking. The Hose Company lost nearly 100 feet of hose due to bursting from the freezing cold but because of their labors, they kept the fire from spreading to nearby buildings.

In any era, lack of funding can determine the success of an enterprise and during this time, the city of Salida still could not financially support the department. So, the Fire Company put out a call for subscriptions:

"It is well known to all of you that our supply of hose is altogether too small for the size of the town, that for want of proper protection from the water, we have inevitably got wet through when we attended fires, to our great discomfort and to the great detriment of our health, and that with our present style of head-gear, we are in constant danger from falling coals and timbers when we go into burning buildings. To protect us from the falling water, coals, etc., we need the regulation rubber coats and the style of helmet usually worn by firemen ... Are there any citizens of the town or members of the council [who] will be liberal enough to subscribe the necessary money?"

Salida responded positively and many local businessmen donated money to the department to keep it running. Over the next few years, the Hose Company survived on subscriptions.

A.T. Ryan, whose livery burned to the ground in January 1883, suffered another disastrous fire later that September, losing both horses and buildings:

"The flames spread with lightning rapidity [and] had wholly enveloped the combustible material in a seething sea of fire ... Too much praise cannot be bestowed upon the firemen, for the courage with which they fought the devouring element, rushing into danger, apparently impelled by the one motive of seeking to save. No earthly power could have saved the building, and they may be proud they stopped the flames when they did. Had it not been a perfectly calm night, there is no telling what the consequences may have been."

Arsonists caused most of the fires in early day Salida and most news articles attributed fires to 'incendiaries.' By the latter part of the 1880s, Salida had seen a fair amount of fire. Two were notable infernos. The 1886 Fire destroyed around 2 blocks between F and G Streets, burning out 31 businesses. The 1888 Fire, which started in Peter Mulvany's hotel that was under construction, took out over 4 blocks, including the corners of F and 2nd Streets, destroying almost sixty businesses. These two massive fires that razed blocks of downtown Salida have been most publicized, but many small business owners lost their entire livelihoods to fires. Many did not have insurance. A November 1884 fire, started by an arsonist, took out Hanley's Millinery Store:

"Mrs. Hanley has had a hard struggle for existence against adverse circumstances in this city, and the loss comes heavy on her, and is very discouraging to one who has suffered as she has the last year. Lynch law is never to be recommended, but if the right party was caught, a rope would relieve the world of a worthless being who could be better spared than kept. A man that will set fire to a house at night is but little better than a midnight assassin."

The Fire Department continued to grow. In November of 1887, an $800 horse-drawn hook and ladder truck had been approved for purchase by City Council. Over $600 of this amount was raised by subscription by the townspeople of Salida.

By the end of the decade, Salidans were becoming realists when it came to fire. The first wooden structures, built in the early 1880s, had been slapdashed together, and by 1890, they were becoming an eyesore. Also, downtown business folks were insuring their properties more so than in the past. A September 1889 fire that took out four saloons on Lower F Street was termed 'a beneficial blaze.' The fire was kept at bay by the Hose Company with assistance from the 'Hook and Ladder boys,' a newly formed wing of the department.

In May of 1890, a large fire at F and 1st Streets, "clean[ed] out some one-story wooden buildings in the heart of the city." It was a calamity that would "prove a blessing to the town" due to the shabby nature of the wooden structures. The properties on F and 1st were becoming valuable due to their location, and as such, owners were more apt to build better: "It is altogether probable that the space will soon be filled up with good substantial brick structures."

A couple of years later, the Salida Fire Department was in danger of being disbanded. During an election for fire warden, City Councilman Wenz made an unsubstantiated attack on one of Salida's bravest. Councilman Wenz "without any good cause whatever" rebuked William Kenton, to whom the entire Fire Department had submitted as their choice for fire warden:

"The boys got hotheaded when they first heard of the abuse of one of their numbers and were very anxious to resign at once, but Capt. Churcher kept them together....The boys will take the steps to reorganize the department if the City Council will interest themselves sufficiently to recognize them as one of the departments of the city."

Later that month, Mayor Wright held a special city council meeting to reestablish the fire department. He thought the department "had been very shabbily treated." In support, he helped raise over $300 to get the department some new quarters on 2nd Street. Things began to settle in for Salida's fire boys.

During the 4th of July celebration of 1892, the Salida Fire Department was "the admiration of everybody, in their new uniforms furnished by Ben Disman." As part of the Independence Day festivities, they competed in a hose race with Buena Vista's Fire Department and handily won the grand prize, a silver trumpet.

By 1900, the building at 124 E Street had been expanded and improved, and became Salida's City Hall, with room for the jail and

the Fire Department's hose house. 124 E Street has since remained the Salida Fire Department's home.

Seven

The Richest & Unluckiest Man in Town

An Irishman with a keen sense for business but beset by the slings and arrows of misfortune was one of Salida's most memorable citizens.

Entrepreneur Peter Mulvany emigrated to Salida in 1880. He purchased some lots on the corner of First and G Streets and put up a two-story building, stocking it with groceries, dry goods, clothing, and provisions aimed for sale to the mining and ranching communities and to the general town populace. Peter was successful, and his sales earnings for 1881 were close to $40,000.

Throughout the decade, Peter added more buildings to his empire on First Street and began selling buggies, phaetons, and wagons, becoming Salida's first vehicle dealership.

Prosperity led to ill luck, and in March 1886, fire destroyed nine of his buildings along with all the contents. Unswayed, Peter quickly rebuilt a new grocery store and accompanying warehouses.

In 1887, Mulvany bought property on the southeast corner of Second and F Streets and began to build a three-story hotel. During this time, his wife Maggie died. Peter worked through his sorrow, and wrote poetry to heal his heart.

His hotel was nearly completed in 1888 when the unopened building caught fire. Flames spread in all four directions, and a third of downtown was razed to the ground. About 60 businesses were lost that day. It was headlined as "The Greatest Fire Salida Ever Saw! ... Black columns of smoke issued from the upper two stories of the Mulvany Hotel and the building which had towered with its three stories, above any business structure in town, stood wrapped in deadly flames ... Many a merchant quailed before what seemed a sure destruction of property on account of lack of water."

A faulty fireplug made for an alarming situation until local Louis Galbraith wrapped himself in a soaked blanket and wrenched open the plug, burning himself in the process. The fire was soon put out but there was no doubt: Louis' heroics saved the rest of downtown that day.

Four days later, a despondent Mulvany placed the following ad in the local paper:

"To the public: Excuse me, [but I] would like to leave. Fellow citizens, buy my goods and property." Mulvany went on to list his business and property holdings and his house, which were all for sale, including the ruins of his hotel. "Thanking my friends for the favors of eight years in business here. I shall now step down and out."

But Salida wasn't letting him get away that easily. The town surrounded and supported Mulvany. One week later: "Peter Mulvany is carrying on an immense grocery trade and it is to be

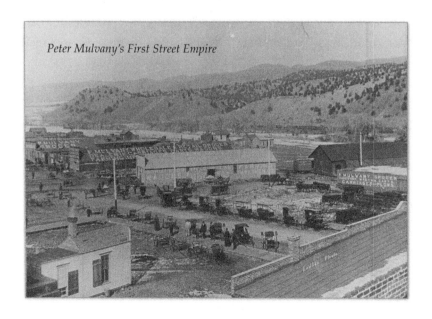

Peter Mulvany's First Street Empire

hoped by all that this enterprising and public-spirited gentleman will decide to remain with us."

Less than two years later, Peter had remarried but once again, he experienced ill luck when fire again took out his grocery stores and warehouses on First Street:

"No business man in Salida has had more disastrous experience from fires than Peter Mulvany. And yet after being burned out three times, he is just as plucky as ever, and will rebuild as soon as possible on a larger scale than before."

By December, Peter built up his grocery store on Second and F and added stock of farm implements, wagons, lumber, and harnesses. It was a real one-stop shop.

Around 1890, Peter suffered through various afflictions, primarily influenza and typhoid fever, which had a crippling effect on him. But in true Mulvany fashion, he bounced back, and a couple of years later could be seen "spinning around Salida in his new top road cart."

For the next seven years, Mulvany's empire prospered, and he expanded it further when he opened a hotel and restaurant in the Union Block, located at 130-138 W. First Street.

But, in December 1897, a blaze struck up and Mulvany again lost a warehouse filled with farming implements on First Street. A spark from a passing engine on the Denver & Rio Grande narrow gauge track was the cause.

An advertisement ran just after: "If you want bargains in scorched goods, call on Peter Mulvany."

Eight

The Capital Contest

In 1881, a referendum was on the state ballot to decide which city in Colorado would get the honor of becoming state capital. Five cities were in the running: Pueblo, Colorado Springs, Canon City, Denver, and Salida.

That spring, the Mountain Mail editorial staff began promoting the town in an effort to garner votes for the election later in the year. Most towns in Colorado were still in a state of formation, and the Mail was optimistic that the bulk of incoming people would settle in the mountains. They were withering in their write-up:

"The capital of the State should be as near to the geographical center of the State as possible, all things considered. The wealth of the State lies in the mountains. The greater portion of the land east of the mountains is a barren waste. The center of population will be west of the plains."

The Mail had reason to be optimistic: Salida was becoming a hub for Denver & Rio Grande Railroad traffic. Trains were coming into Salida and dispersing to every direction in the state: east to Pueblo, north to Leadville, west to Gunnison, and south into the San Luis

Valley: "Take a map of the State and trace out all these lines and it will be seen that Salida can be more easily reached by people living in all parts of the State than any other town," and this was true enough.

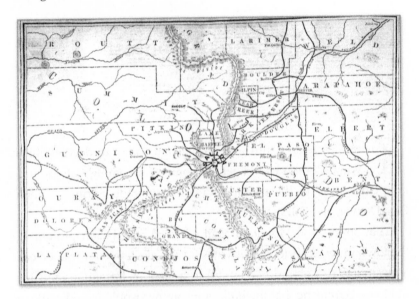

Editorials appeared all during the campaign season that autumn, touting Salida and decrying the claims of the other contenders.

Colorado Springs ran on the claim that it was a temperance town since it had no licensed saloons, but the Mail editor argued: "The difference between Colorado Springs and other towns on the temperance question is this: In other places the whiskey seller procures a license; in Colorado Springs, he don't."

Denver was accused of buying the vote: "Denver's uneasiness on the capital question is shown by the large number of emissaries she has sent through the state. Denver's corruption fund must be immense."

Out in the barren wastes, "Pueblo bases her claim on the expectation (expectation, mind you) of being the future, great commercial center of the State. It is hardly worthwhile to waste space in calling attention to the utter imbecility of voting for a point on the ground of expectation."

And Canon City became disgruntled once they saw the distorted map, and accused Salida of being "land grabbers." The Mountain Mail responded: "The [Canon City] Reporter refers to land grabbers with a great flourish of trumpets ... The land project in connection with Salida and the state capital is an honorable and straightforward business proposition. If the Reporter would take the trouble to investigate before it shoots off its mouth, it would not act so as to appear so ridiculous."

It soon became clear that the Mail editorials were simply tourism boosters for our town rather than serious plays for capital contention:

"There is probably no point in the State so favorably situated, all things considered, as Salida ... If people could live on scenery, we could glut the market of the world. The gulches and canons in the neighborhood of Salida are more rugged, more beautiful, and more attractive, and within sight of the doors of every cottage in Salida. There are ten mountains that raise their hoary peaks hundreds of feet nearer heaven than does proud old Pike, the sentinel of the plains. The mineral springs in the vicinity of Salida far surpass those found elsewhere in the State. Six miles down the river from Salida, and within two hundred yards of the railroad track, are the famous warm springs owned by Mr. Wells. The water as it flows from the ground is of just the right temperature for bathing purposes, and a plunge bath can be had there that will cheer, that will invigorate, and that will cure. The waters of the hot springs at Poncha, the beautiful little village at the foot of Poncha Pass and five miles from Salida, are noted for their curative properties."

On November 8, votes were cast in the general election on the capital question. The vote was lopsided in favor of Denver, which received over 30,000 votes. Pueblo, Colorado Springs, and Canon City received votes in the low thousands, and Salida came in a disappointing last, receiving 695. Afterwards, the following appeared in the Mountain Mail:

"Salida didn't care anything about [the referendum] anyhow. She only made the race for the purpose of bringing herself in to prominence and to see whether her neighbors would really be neighborly or not. She succeeded in both. Her location and advantages have been more extensively advertised than they possibly could have been in any other manner. It has brought business men and families here who will stay. And in the matter of finding out how neighborly her neighbors were she has been successful. To her friends in Poncha Springs, Maysville, and other points in the South Arkansas Valley she makes her most profound acknowledgments."

Nine

Rise of the Cattle Thieves

In the early 1880s, cattle theft was not only big business in Salida, but also the South Park, Gunnison, Saguache, and Canon City areas. Illegal meat markets had set up near mines and towns and cattle thieves freely spent their ill-gotten earnings in the local settlements and mining camps.

In the spring of 1883, a rancher by the name of Henderson had a small herd of about 20 cattle pastured around Pass Creek, near Poncha Springs. Over a span of several months, cattle thieves stole every single one of his cows. Henderson witnessed his last cow being killed by two men and, being alone, he left to get some neighbors to confront the thieves. They had left by the time he returned and a posse was rounded up, but the cattle thieves were never caught. This report was not an isolated incident. There was a rustling epidemic occurring in the Salida area.

In 1865, Baxter Stingley was 25 when he moved to Colorado Territory from Iowa. He worked at various odd jobs in the area, mining or bartending. In November of 1880, Baxter filled in as Salida's temporary marshal for about a month, gaining some experience in law enforcement. A year later he was appointed deputy marshal of Salida. Two weeks into his job, the town marshal had resigned and Salida appointed Baxter as marshal of Salida, for which he received a monthly salary of $75.

Baxter took his job seriously. Concealed weapons were illegal in Salida, and it was a tough business trying to keep the peace in the freshly minted state of Colorado, still somewhat lawless in its hidden corners. Guns were relatively expensive but the Civil War had created a more pervasive environment for gun ownership. People coming out west were armed for hunting and for protection:

"Baxter Stingley, town marshal, says that persons who are in the habit of carrying concealed weapons had better look out. He is going to pull every mother's son of them." That's some swearing, 1880s style.

At the end of May 1883, Tom Ninemire and Tom Evans came prowling into town from Brown's Canon to steal some cattle: "There are persons in Salida today who say that they heard some of the gang say before they left the coal kilns that they were going down the river on a hunt, but that they would stop in Salida on the way down and clean out the town."

Ninemire and Evans weren't the most savory of characters. Tom Evans had boasted to friends: "I'd like to see the son of a bitch's face who can arrest me." And Ninemire was still smarting from a grudge he was holding with Salida law enforcement. A month earlier a prostitute had stolen money from him but with no proof, Marshal Stingley could not compel the woman to return the money. Ninemire was out for revenge.

Once Ninemire and Evans got to town, they proceeded to Bender's Saloon and Boarding House. At Bender's, described as a "hole of iniquity," the pair began getting drunk and disorderly. As a result, Marshal Stingley and Deputy James Bathurst were called in to the saloon to dispense some peace. That's when things went south. Ninemire pulled a gun and began shooting at both officers. Stingley and Bathurst returned fire. Bullets were flying from both sides as bar patrons scattered. Evans pulled a knife and attempted to stab Bathurst before he was shot and killed by the deputy. A bar patron was shot and killed trying to get out of the way. Shots fired by Ninemire hit Bathurst in the chest and Stingley in the thigh and chest. Luckily, Stingley happened to have a watch in his left vest pocket that deflected this second bullet. Ninemire escaped out the back, shooting a path clear:

"Ninemire started up 1st street toward Devereux's. Chris Laub tried to intercept him and was fired at for his pains, as also was A.T. Ryan. Ninemire ran out past A.T. Ryan's stable and Moody's lumber yard, and by this time fifty men or more were after him with revolvers, rifles, shotguns, and every other conceivable kind of weapon that could be found. As they pursued him and fired, he returned the salute. Among the pursuers was W.H. Brown, a teamster, who had borrowed a gun and was on horseback. He had reached to within [15 feet] of Ninemire where the latter was on the mesa north of the railroad track and not far from William Van Every's residence. Here Ninemire turned and deliberately shot Brown off of his horse and was attempting to capture the horse and mount him when the pursuing party captured him and brought him into town. Talk of lynching Ninemire was freely indulged in by some of Salida's best citizens, and had one man taken the lead, and said 'Come on, boys' Ninemire's body would have been dangling at the end of a rope in less than ten minutes."

Baxter Stingley's watch is housed at the Salida Museum.

Stingley recovered from his wounds but four people died that day, including Deputy Marshal Bathurst.

A tribute to James Bathurst appeared the following week, reprinted in part here:

"In business, his word was an early execution of a promise, a promise not put aside and never unfulfilled. He was a friend under all circumstances, on all sorts of occasions, and in all sorts of ways.

He never ceased an untiring and constant devotion to those he loved and admired. His bravery was proverbial with those who knew him, and to his death he marched with unfaltering tread and met it with no emotion of fear or restraint."

Ninemire was convicted for the murder of Bathurst but spent less than a year in the Buena Vista Jail before escaping the next January. He was never recaptured.

Ten

The Lynching of Lauren 'Ed' Watkins

On July 6, 1883, cattle thieves struck in the mountains of Chaffee County:

"This week the communities of St. Elmo and Tin Cup have been somewhat stirred up over a raid by officers from outside counties after cattle thieves. On Thursday, they made a dash on William McGuire, proprietor of the Tin Cup meat market, and Mr. McGuire now languishes in the Gunnison jail. It appears that one of the beeves he butchered wore a hide upon which was the brand of the widow woman who runs the Tin Cup dairy. [Not only was McGuire arrested but] the Christison brothers, William Taylor, and Frank Reed were as well … Considerable talk about cattle thieves has been indulged in about Salida and Poncha lately."

During this time the local paper was printing ads offering cash rewards, in some cases as high as $1,000, for the arrest and conviction of parties stealing cattle and horses from ranches ranging from South Park to Canon City to Saguache.

Closer to home, a man named Lauren 'Ed' Watkins had a ranch and slaughterhouse at Badger Creek, just below Whitehorn, which is 15 miles northeast of Salida. Watkins held roundups and marketed cattle on his ranch. He did good business in Salida, selling meat to the local butchers.

Suspicions were rife with the cattle owners in the area, particularly the South Park ranchers. Most of them suspected Watkins of rustling. Ranch hand John Hyssong worked for the Ira Mulock Ranch in South Park and was given a mission by his boss. He got a job at Watkins' place, punching cows. But he was also an undercover spy, and set out to find the truth of the matter. John remembers the charm of Watkins:

"Watkins was 29, suave, and good-looking, large and gracious, a big spender at roundup time. He had a good-sized following, was married to a former schoolteacher, and had considerable influence in Salida. He could shoot the eye out of a rabbit as far as he could see the animal. He never pulled a trigger. He cocked his six-shooter with his thumb and let 'er go."

Watkins cut a romantic figure, but was he a cattle thief? It looked likely. Hyssong witnessed firsthand the criminal activity that was occurring at Watkins' place. At the direction of Watkins, cattle and horses were being stolen and their brands disfigured. And among his known associates was Frank Reed.

Once Hyssong returned to the IM Ranch to tell his tale, things were set in motion. Within a few days, around twenty armed cattlemen and their cowboys showed up on Watkins' doorstep demanding their stock back. Sure of himself, Watkins showed them the cattle but the ranchers, being unsatisfied with his branding methods, forcefully took around 20 head and left.

Watkins immediately filed suit against the South Park ranchers to get the cattle back: "The cattle taken were the property of Mr. Watkins, and he is able to show where they came from and make good his claim. Mr. Watkins has brought suit by replevin for the cattle, and has also brought suit in the name of the State against the parties for stealing the cattle."

Salida townsfolk remained ignorant of Watkins' true nature but the ranchers knew who they were dealing with. They meted out swift justice on Watkins.

A week later on August 11, Watkins was in Canon City to answer the charges against him and to post a $4,000 bond. He was in the company of the Fremont County sheriff when both were overwhelmed by vigilantes:

"The night was extremely dark and alighting from the train, Sheriff Jones and Watkins walked hurriedly up through town to the jail. Entering the courthouse yard, a few steps brought the pair to the corner, where from 14 to 16 masked men were concealed in an angle of the building. In the inky darkness that prevailed, the first intimation of their presence was revealed when in deep silence they seized Sheriff Jones, and pinioned [with cord] his arms behind him … The mob then sped away in pursuit of Watkins and the heavy tramp of men in rapid motion was the only sound heard for a few moments until a sharp crack of a pistol rang out in the darkness and silence reigned again. Sheriff Jones regained his feet and reaching the door of his residence, was admitted by his daughter who cut the cords that had secured his arms. He then took a lantern and vainly searched all the surrounding premises for those who had participated in the outrage."

In an era before street lamps, Sheriff Jones was unable to locate Watkins, but with the coming of the sun, Jones found his body swinging from the 'west end bridge.'

The Mountain Mail newspaper was stunned: "This reveals the act of the dastards ... The lynching of L.E. Watkins at Canon City was a cold blooded, premeditated murder in every sense, and the perpetrators, who by their action have cast a stain upon Canon City's fair fame, should be hunted down and given the full benefit of the law. It was by no means proven that Watkins was a cattle thief; on the contrary we are inclined to believe that he was innocent of the charge."

The next day there was a town meeting held at the opera house here in Salida, which was part candlelight vigil, part rabble rouse. Many Salidans attended the event and "Judge Garrison was called for. [He] delivered the rousing speech of the evening, testifying, as all the speakers did, to the unimpeachable character of Mr. Watkins, and condemning in the most scathing language the cowardly action of mobocracy." It was getting a little frenzied in Salida.

A few days later, the ranchers who were being litigated by the now deceased Watkins appeared for their day in Salida court, and a crowd of over 200 armed and angry Salidans surrounded them at the Denver & Rio Grande train station, threatening them with retaliation for the murder of Watkins. The ranchers made it to court and conducted their business but afterwards it was mob mentality in the streets of Salida, with armed men taunting and provoking the South Park ranchers. Things could have gone badly but for the calming presence of Marshal Baxter Stingley, who quietly ushered the South Park ranchers back to the railroad station, thus averting a bloodbath in the streets of Salida. The charges against the South Park ranchers were later dismissed.

A few weeks later, the Cattle Grower's Convention met in Poncha Springs and set the record straight:

"There has existed in Chaffee County for several years an organized gang of cattle thieves, who have stolen cattle from the cattle owners and ranchmen of the Arkansas Valley and off the Cameron hills along the southwest limits of the South Park, until over $200,000 worth of cattle have been taken or driven out of Chaffee County alone. These depredations were at first committed secretly, a few head of stock being driven off or killed in some remote mountain fastness and then the meat marketed through some friendly butcher shops in the nearest valley towns and mining camps. But of late, immunity from punishment has so emboldened the thieves that they have driven from these ranges entire bunches of cattle and horses and disfigured and altered their brands, and then have driven them at leisure across the county, inviting inspection and challenging discovery. When the lawful owners of the cattle with disfigured brands [which were discovered in Watkins' possession] claimed the cattle, he disputed their title, and refused to give them up, and when the owners drove them off he had the audacity to go to Salida and swear out warrants for the arrest of the owners of the cattle, notwithstanding the fact that he, himself, was under arrest, but out on bail, for stealing the same cattle. As to the lynching of Watkins, the cattle and ranch men and the best citizens of this section of the country are unanimous in giving expression to a sense of relief at his 'removal' from the ranges in this vicinity."

Salida was sufficiently chastened by the closing lines:

"It is to be regretted that the public has been misinformed through the activity and shrewdness of Watkins' friends, the parties most interested in first gaining the ear of the press, as to the real condition of affairs culminating in his death at Canon City."

Eleven

The Murder of Baxter Stingley

In September of 1883, Marshal Baxter Stingley was running for sheriff of Chaffee County. He ran an ad in the local paper:

"Baxter Stingley wishes to inform the public that he is running for sheriff on his own merits alone, regardless of anybody. He would like the office, but has no money to buy it, and the support of his friends will be thankfully received."

On September 14th, Frank Reed and Bent Jamison came to town "armed to the teeth." Since carrying a concealed weapon was prohibited in Salida, Marshal Stingley confronted the pair and requested they either put aside their guns or leave town. Reed and Jamison complied and were getting ready to leave town, when a warrant was handed off to Baxter. Bent Jamison was wanted in Saguache County:

"Knowing Jamison and Reed were about to leave town, Marshal Stingley hastily summoned his deputy, Mr. Frizelle, and went to where the men were getting their horses. Stingley approached him and said: 'Bent, I have a warrant for you,' at the same time having his hands in the pockets of [his] coat – one on the warrant and the other on a small pistol. Jamison replied: 'I will never be taken alive,' and then drew a .45. Stingley's first impulse was to shoot through his pocket; but, casting his eye over his shoulder, he discovered Reed, very near, with a cocked Winchester leveled on Frizelle and himself, and he knew if he fired at Jamison, certain death awaited him, and perhaps, his deputy as well. Seeing no opportunity for either himself or his deputy to make a movement, Marshal Stingley left, and ran down the street for a shotgun and help, but the cowboys were too quick for him and hastily rode away."

Certain things can be surmised from this encounter. Frank Reed and Bent Jamison were known associates of the cattle thief L.E. Watkins, who had been lynched a month prior. There would have been rumblings of anger amongst the thieves since their syndicate of cattle rustling had been broken up. Reed had told friends that he would "never be taken alive," a popular catchphrase amongst outlaws. Perhaps Baxter caught some hell for his actions. Did some of Salida's citizens consider their marshal cowardly because he ran away from armed men? Baxter considered the safety of himself and his deputy and weighed it against issuing a warrant but who can say what was going on in his mind? Perhaps he would be more reckless in his next encounter with the outlaws. At any rate, the editors at the local paper had his back:

"Salida has been infested with a gang of thieves and burglars, but the visits of this class of citizens are few and far between. Our police force, headed by our efficient marshal, Baxter Stingley, usually drop onto a gang as soon as they come to the city and their stay is short. Ornamenting the end of a rope has no charm in their eyes."

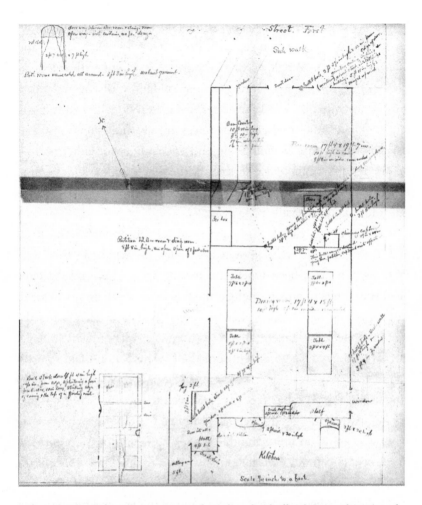

A rendering of the crime scene at Arbor's by a local official. It is a footprint of the restaurant and plots the bullet holes in the walls. A total of ten can be counted, which, of course, does not include those that entered bodies.

Things came to a head on Sunday, October 28th. Baxter had a warrant for Frank Reed on a charge of cattle theft and he had heard news that Frank and his gang were hanging out at Arbor's Variety and Dance Hall, down on First Street. Baxter armed himself with his two pistols (one a .44 caliber English Bulldog, the other a Colt .45) and set out towards Arbor's to confront Reed. Once inside, he pulled the Bulldog and said "Frank, I have a warrant for you, throw up your hands." Reed hesitated with his hands in his pockets, then "quick as lightning" pulled a gun on Baxter. One shot hit Baxter, and then they both exchanged multiple shots. Reed ran out the back door, all the while firing his gun at Baxter. Baxter was close behind but at the door he stopped, and collapsed. He was mortally wounded. Placed on a table in the dance hall's back room, he bled profusely, enough so that his "boots were filled with blood." He died soon after.

Frank Reed must have been shot as well but not enough to deter him. Once he was outside, he fired one more shot to keep the crowd back, and then escaped.

That Sunday was a sad day here in Salida: "The very atmosphere today appears burdened with gloom and sadness of the death of Marshal Stingley ... For the killing of Baxter no one is to blame except the man who did the shooting. Baxter was right and the [Mountain] Mail takes those grounds against the friends of Frank Reed, who are silently gloating over his death. May these *friends* of Reed and gang meet the just retribution they deserve. Reed was sent for by a gang to kill Baxter. For Reed, hanging is too good. ... Baxter was universally respected and well thought of by everybody that knew him. His death is a sad blow to his many friends, his brother, father, and sister. May a just God do things well. Peace to the ashes of

Baxter Stingley. Salida is sad. A man with a heart as big as an ox has been ushered into the great hereafter."

A witness to the event later reported that Baxter was essentially "committing suicide" by going into Arbor's and issuing the warrant. Perhaps, but a marshal's job was to serve warrants and protect the peace. At the very least, Baxter's actions demonstrate that he was dedicated to his job and to the citizens of Salida. In the two years that Baxter was marshal it was decidedly the most dangerous time to be a police officer in Salida.

City Council immediately approved a $1,000 reward "to be paid to the person or persons bringing and delivering the body of Frank Reed into the hands of the officers of the town of Salida, or to the Sheriff of Chaffee County." Eventually, $3,500 in total would be offered as reward. In later years, Reed was spotted in Arizona, Indiana, Illinois, Texas, and Colorado but he was never captured.

Baxter Stingley had a distinguished funeral ceremony with the town band, the Salida Fire Department, and "several secret societies" all accompanying his body to the Cleora Cemetery where he was buried.

His stone has since been lost to time, possibly due to the fact that a gold bearing vein was discovered in the cemetery in 1894. Prospectors were given free rein to go in as the "property was capable of being worked to great profit."

Twelve

Charles Rush's Memories of Leadville

"I doubt very much that there would be a Salida or a railroad here today except for the boom in 1878 when people were almost crazy about the fabulous wealth hidden in the hills around California Gulch, which is known as Leadville today, the greatest silver mining camp in the world, at that time."

So begins a manuscript written by Charles Rush, a reminiscence of his early years growing up in the Salida and Leadville areas. An only child, Rush grew up at Brown's Canon, close to where Stone Bridge is today, in a section house which his parents ran. After his father was murdered by a track walker (a person who maintains the line), Rush had to go to work. He was 16 years old.

He got his first job in 1886 surveying a line to Aspen for the Colorado Midland Railroad:

"The survey party ran the line from Hagerman Tunnel to Lime Creek. It was a tough job and dangerous besides. Ropes had to be used to let yourself down the steep walls of [Hell's Gate] Canon. You had to take your boots off to go down in your stocking feet, tie your rope to a tree or a large boulder and hang on to the rope. The surveyor's instruments were let down on a kind of sled made out of jack pine ... Hell's Gate was rightly named – it was a hell of place and a hell of place to have to build a railroad."

After the surveying job was complete, Rush got a job with the D&RG doing grunt work on the engines. He lived and worked in Leadville, which, at the time, was jumping. There were an estimated 15,000 people there in 1880; by 1893, before the Silver Panic, the population was at over 40,000. Life in Leadville was rough: miners were scrabbling for gold, and everybody else was scrabbling for some of the money from that gold profit. Here's Rush, describing Leadville:

"The underworld was in full blast – two blocks of them – gambling joints, saloons, variety theatres, dance halls, and hop joints. Forty-five thousand people within a radius of two miles: Chestnut Street, Harrison Avenue, and State Street thronged with people. Lots of money, lots of whiskey, lots of girls, and lots of killings and deaths from diseases, gun battles, and lynchings. The cemetery on lower Chestnut Street had 1,500 bodies in it in a year's time.

"The law in that town, or hellhole, was two colt .45s and fifty feet of lynch hemp rope with 100 or more good civilians to handle it and those that did not know much about a .45 learned how to tie a necktie around the neck of the offender in short order. The worst drawback was a good place to hold the ropes.

"Almost daily the body of some poor unfortunate would be found in a shallow shaft or the back door of some saloon. I lived not far from the old cemetery on lower Chestnut where they dug up the body of a woman, took off her clothes and resold the coffin. Then they dragged her body back in the grave. You were not safe even after you were dead in Leadville."

After this daunting education, Rush finally got the promotion he was waiting for: engine fireman for the Denver & Rio Grande. He was just 23. Some of his responsibilities included working a switch engine, which was a small engine that moved railroad cars around the rail yard, and various other tasks related to keeping an engine in working order. His most important task: "fire the engine, keep it hot, and don't let it pop."

Five years later, Rush's greatest desire came true: he was promoted to engineer:

"I was assigned to engine 106. With my new suit of overalls, new cap, new gloves, with cuffs and a star on them, a new watch, and a gaudy gold chain, I thought everybody was watching me (or should), especially the girls who passed by."

Rush worked for the Denver & Rio Grande for 51 years. For 46 of those years he was a railroad engineer, based out of Salida.

Thirteen

The Cochetopa Forest

The Cochetopa Forest was established in June 1905 by Theodore Roosevelt, our most forward-thinking President on matters of land conservation. The Cochetopa (Ute for 'little island') encompassed 900,000 acres, and this forest was, in later years, parceled up to become the San Isabel, Gunnison, and Rio Grande Forests.

Lumber was a plentiful resource during the westward expansion and regulation was lax in the matter of harvesting it. The boom of railroad building took an estimated 25% of U.S. lumber for railroad ties. The need for charcoal to fire the smelters was of importance to the mining community. Charcoal is a fuel that burns hotter than wood, so it is a more efficient means of smelting mineral content from ore.

Denver & Rio Grande engineer Charles Rush grew up and worked in Brown's Canon. He describes the charcoal industry here:

"Wood choppers, kiln fillers, burner haulers, and charcoal loaders (about 200 all told) were employed at Brown's Canon. Charcoal burning was the largest industry in the Arkansas Valley ... The timber was all cut off for props and lagging for the mines. It was cut to make charcoal for the smelters. What was left (of the trees) was killed by the smoke and gas from the furnaces that smelted the ore."

The Denver & Rio Grande Railroad made certain that timber, and the charcoal made from that timber, would be big business in Chaffee County:

"About 1880, following the mining boom in and around Leadville, there was a big demand for charcoal used in smelting the ore and charcoal kilns were started in operation throughout the country. Kilns were installed at Riverside, Cleora, Poncha Springs, and other points along the Arkansas River. Large quantities of piñon were converted into charcoal and rather extensive areas were completely denuded of this timber. The D&RG station above Poncha Springs is still known as Charcoal Spur."

Railroad ties ready for transport

Charcoal kilns were serious, sturdy structures built for their task. Charles Rush describes the kilns as being "built out of brick, 25 to 30 feet in diameter at the bottom, cone-shaped or like a beehive, about 20 to 25 feet high, a loading door at the top, unloading door at the bottom. Each kiln held about 100 cords of wood. It took 7 or 8 days to make the charcoal. One or two men had to be on continuous watch to see that the right draft [came] from the port holes, to char the wood uniformly. Piñon was the best wood for charcoal and brought a bigger price at the smelters."

All of this cutting and burning began to take its toll on the forest but not many would take up the banner for forest defense. When money is involved, industry tends to get ravenous.

Edgar T. Ensign, Colorado's first Forest Commissioner who was based in Colorado Springs, wrote an impassioned *Plea for Rocky Mountain Forests*:

"Railway building in the Rocky Mountain region, especially in Colorado, is increasing in such rapid proportion as to offer a most serious menace to the existence of the forests. After the tie-chopping legion come settlers, miners, lumbermen, charcoal burners, and others, all of whom, in addition to the havoc wrought by themselves, prepare the way for that most dreaded of all enemies – fire. The demand of the railways for cross-ties, timber, and dimension lumber causes the most serious drain upon the forest. For ties, only the young, partly-grown and most vigorous trees are used; the consumption for that purpose alone is enormous."

Remnants of the exploitation are still visible today. On Woodchopper's Trail, the old stumps average about 3 feet high, the level at which a saw was used. Evidence of old saw mills can also be seen elsewhere around the county. There's a notable one near the Colorado Trail intersection on road 267 near Tin Cup Pass.

With all this use of kilns, smelters, home fireplaces and cook stoves, not to mention the railroad, there must have been extensive pollution in Chaffee County. Throw in a little inversion, and it would have become a toxic soup.

The damage done may be most visible today when one looks at Tenderfoot Mountain. The EPA's Smeltertown report states that there was serious vegetative destruction from the smelter emissions, which could account for the lack of trees on Tenderfoot.

Fourteen

Granite's Early Days

In 1859, a few "adventurous spirits" discovered gold in Clear Creek just west of Denver and triggered a Colorado gold rush, "inflaming the imaginations of their companions." By the following year, miners had spread into the mountains west of Denver seeking their fortune. Two of the places that they settled in was Cache Creek, and then Granite, the first two towns established in Lake County. Lake County was considerably larger back then, reaching to the western edge of the state; Chaffee County didn't splinter off until 1879.

Miners extracted these first traces of gold through placer mining, essentially mining directly into the stream beds of creeks. This extensive placer mining depleted the quantities of gold rapidly.

R.G. Dill wrote about the rush during these early days:

"The excitement that followed these then wonderful discoveries was intense. In the summer of 1860, the population of Denver had reached nearly 4,000, and probably as many more were scattered about in the various gulches in which gold had been found. The discovery of these diggings, the richest yet found, and therefore

named California Gulch, soon reached Denver and the neighboring camps. As a result, a universal rush for California Gulch was inaugurated ... The fortunate first-comers were reported to be taking out gold by the handful. In the fall of 1860, there were not less than 10,000 people in the gulch, and from the foot of the gulch near the present site of the town of Malta, every foot was taken up, the lines extending from bank to bank."

By 1860, the town of Granite had established itself as a supply point for the miners at Cache Creek and the surrounding area. It soon had a thriving population of 300 and its own post office.

After a year or so the stream beds were depleted and an exodus of sorts happened around California Gulch. Most of the small settlement towns that had sprung up were abandoned. But Granite remained an outpost for the miners who stayed.

When the Yankee Blade and Amizette lode deposits were discovered in 1867, Granite flourished. Several more veins were discovered and mining companies set up shop, investing in stamp mills (machines that crush ore) to get to the gold. By 1900, millions of dollars in gold had been mined out of the Granite area. Granite continued to produce large deposits of gold until around 1920.

One of the families who came to Colorado in search of that gold were the Bradburys. Originally from Illinois, patriarch Samuel Bradbury mined around Gunnison, Gothic City, and Garfield. His grandson Frank also took up mining, and mined lodes near Turret, Aspen, and other areas in the region. By 1900, Frank had settled with his wife and family in Granite. And in 1908, Frank discovered $125 ore in the Margeret Mine he operated:

"A remarkable feature of the discovery is the fact that the ore was found very near the surface ... It carries about 10% lead and considerable silver. There is free gold in such quantities in certain parts of the ore that it can easily be seen. In patches the ore is so rich that it will assay about $2,000 per ton. The vein that has been opened in the Margeret is a continuation of the streak that was struck in the old Yankee Blade property many years ago."

Frank Bradbury worked in nearly every mine in the Granite area and continued working well into his 80s. He died in Granite in 1956.

Today, Granite thrives with a population of about 100. Tourists are still drawn to the placer creeks west of town, looking for remnants of gold.

Fifteen

Ghosts of the Alpine Tunnel

The push to lay rail westward hit a fever pitch in Colorado in the 1880s. To that end, the Denver, South Park, & Pacific Railroad made a plan to build a railway tunnel in the high mountains of Colorado. In January of 1880, they began the long process of digging a passage to and then through the Continental Divide. By August, the DSP&P was advertising for 1,000 men to work on the Alpine Tunnel. Men, of all races, answered the call.

It took a year and a half to move earth, blast rock, and construct rail bed. In July 1881, the Gunnison Daily News-Democrat newspaper made the announcement: "The Rockies Pierced: Daylight Breaks through the Denver & South Park Railway Tunnel."

Who would be the first person to go through? The tunnel crew conferred and all agreed: DSP&P Superintendent Osborne's child was the first to walk through the gap that would become the Alpine Tunnel. Chief Engineer Barr had to pony up $10 before he could pass through. This money was well spent on beer for the workers.

Hundreds of men dug, blasted, and scraped out this passage through the Rockies. It would take another year before the tunnel sides were shored up and track was laid. In that time, at least three men died during building. In July 1881, a munitions worker was blasting in the tunnel when a mass of powder discharged in front of him. He was killed instantly. And in October of 1881, while tunnel workers were excavating, a large boulder dislodged and fell, killing two.

Notably, there were two instances of murder at the Tunnel. One man shot and killed a fellow worker after a drunken quarrel. He was acquitted of the crime.

The other was not so fortunate. After an argument involving money, Thomas Coleman shot and killed Andrew Smith, a fellow railway worker. Though Coleman proclaimed it was a case of self-defense, he was judged and found guilty. On the evening before his death, he was attended by several women. A writer for the Gunnison Daily News-Democrat was there to witness. The scene was piercing:

"A moment later a group of colored women entered the room. As they did so, the condemned man approached the grating and extended his fingers through the bars. One old woman seized the extended hand, and with soft, motherly words tried to cheer and comfort him.

"'I sent for you,' he said slowly, 'I wanted to thank you for coming to see me last night. It was the first time that any of my own people had come near me since I have been here ... Will you be at my execution?' he faltered."

When the old woman responded in the affirmative, Coleman continued: "'I'm glad of that, and I want to ask you to sing and pray for me.'"

His hanging was a gruesome spectacle, not only because of the situation but also due to a faulty trap door that prolonged the agony:

"The suspense was awful, while Coleman cried, 'What is the matter? Why don't they kill me?' ... The platform was cleared, the signal was given, and Coleman was swung into eternity." After he was cut down, the crowd closed in to see his remains, and then fought over pieces of the rope. It was Gunnison's first public execution.

The tunnel was not cheap to build. Besides the cost of manpower, a premium California redwood was used in shoring up the tunnel interior. Heart redwood is a high-grade, durable wood which is resistant to rot. Eighty years after the tunnel was built, Dow Helmers dug into the Tunnel to investigate and he snapped some photos showing it to be fairly intact. These images can be seen in his definitive book, *Historic Alpine Tunnel.* Estimates vary but it is safe to put a price of $300,000 - $400,000 on the building of the tunnel. In today's dollars, $300,000 would be around $7.5 million.

Hopes were high in 1882 for train service to begin. The Leadville Daily Herald reported: "The South Park branch of the Union Pacific is preparing for a grand excursion season [this] coming summer. The Gunnison branch beyond the Alpine Tunnel will be the most attractive place, besides one of the most romantic places in the mountains."

On July 13, 1882, the first train came through the Alpine Tunnel. Newspaperman C.F.R. Hayward recalled the experience: "Chalk Creek valley, with its pine-clad slopes, stretches away to the South, abruptly ending its green way against a mountain range that stands barrier-like thirty miles distant. To the west, a granite wall. Suddenly the valley, mountain peaks, and blue sky disappear. A blackness, darker than the night, permeates everything ... Another metamorphosis. Night has gone and day has come again. To the east, a granite wall. To the west, a wooded valley, with sparkling streams threading their way through it like flashes of sunlight."

At an altitude of 11,500 feet, the Alpine Tunnel was the highest railway tunnel in North America and Europe. It spanned over 1,700 feet in length and had a height of 17 feet. It is estimated that 450,000 feet of Heart California redwood was used to shore up the interior.

A week later, the railway had built track to the tiny hamlet of Pitkin. The Elk Mountain Pilot documented the day:

"About noon on Wednesday, the tracklayers reached the town site, and at 3:30 p.m., the track was laid to the depot, and at four o'clock a construction train was run down into town amid cheers, firing of guns, and the playing of Pitkin's cornet band. Almost the entire population turned out to greet the iron horse, and the enthusiasm and rejoicing showed it to be the greatest day within the history of Pitkin town. Several hundred people were upon the ground. Kegs of beer and boxes of cigars had been placed near the track by Mayor Williams and other citizens and after a well-appointed address of welcome by Lawyer Drexilius, work was stopped and the entire railroad force invited to refreshments."

The Alpine Tunnel had been operational for a couple of years when a series of disasters occurred. In 1884, an avalanche swept down and completely engulfed the town of Woodstock, a small station just past the west side of the Alpine Tunnel. Not many people lived there, just fourteen, but the town was decimated. Thirteen were killed in the slide; just one man escaped:

"The depot building, section house and three residences, in the line of the slide, were swept from the face of the mountain and carried with the moving mass of snow a thousand feet to the valley below, and so deeply covered that it will take weeks to shovel down."

Thirty-five feet of snow, trees, and rocks covered the railroad track. A train's snow wedge made no difference here; only dynamite and hand digging would clear the track. It was the first evidence of the high cost of keeping the Tunnel open.

In January of 1885, a train passing through the Tunnel had the misfortune of coming out into a snow bank, effectively trapping it. One passenger, by the name of Rohlfing, was aboard the ill-fated train and decided to make the trek back into Buena Vista to get help.

Thinking that some of the station houses along the way would be open so he could warm up and get help, he proceeded towards his destination, 40 miles distant. Unbeknownst to Rohlfing, every station house along the route was closed, so he had no choice but to keep walking through the snow, averaging about a mile an hour. Partway through his journey, he slipped and fell through a train trestle and landed in the creek below. He later remarked: "I have taken cold baths, but nothing that ever compared with that."

Struggling in the snow now with a sprained ankle, he was close to giving up, but courage rising, he crawled to the top of the embankment and limped off towards Buena Vista. Rohlfing recalled:

"I was frequently inclined to lay down and take a friendly nap with the snow, but realizing that the frost was getting me under its influence, I walked on. Finally, upon the afternoon of the second day, I arrived at the depot in Buena Vista, and of all the tough looking transients that ever you saw, I was the one. I couldn't have walked another mile to have saved my life, and how I ever got through the snow drifts, with a sprained ankle, and conquered the blizzards, is something that I'll never know."

Snow and rock slides and the constant expense for men to clear the rail line resulted in the Denver, South Park, and Pacific Railroad going bankrupt. The track was abandoned in 1890 and the Tunnel lay in disuse for about five years.

In 1895, the DSP&P reorganized and became the Denver, Leadville, and Gunnison Railway Company. With the new company came a new dream of reopening the Tunnel. That June, a correspondent for the Denver Post wrote optimistically, and a little ironically: "In its construction is seen one of the greatest triumphs of man over the difficulties of nature. Wild streams, yawning chasms, dizzy heights, have all been overcome and for more than fourteen years the iron horse has traveled over a firm road-bed carrying men through the mountain wilds with ease and safety."

But the reopening came with a cost. When the Tunnel was built in 1881, each side, east and west, were constructed to slope down from the middle, the center of the Tunnel being the highest point. In early June 1895, as an engine was backing cars into the Tunnel, the front car became detached and raced backwards down the incline. Thirteen men leapt from the speeding cars; two were killed.

Later that June, four workers had entered in from the east side to begin clearing the blocked Tunnel and were working in a small opening on the inside. The blockage had dammed up water from passing rain storms which had no way to drain from the Tunnel. An engine was brought in to pump the water out. When the scorching firebox on the engine came into proximity with the water, clouds of gas and vapor formed, choking the men. With no way out, the engineer attempted a final ditch effort to ram the train engine through to the west side of the Tunnel (still partially blocked by rock fall) to create a gap in the Tunnel to let the toxic vapors escape. It was unsuccessful. Four men died including the engineer, 'Dad' Martenis, who was found dead with his hand still on the throttle.

Trains ran until 1910, when the Alpine Tunnel was abandoned. As time passes, the stones erode, timbers break, water seeps, ice cracks, and snow melts. This degradation continues to wear down the Tunnel and the roads leading up to it on both sides of the Divide. But it still draws tourists and locals alike who want to witness the engineering efforts of those railroad laborers who unwittingly created a memorial to themselves.

Sixteen

Electric Salida

On December 8, 1887, the evening gloom scattered when the Edison Electric Light Company lighted the first location in Salida:

"The incandescent lamps that were lighted on F St. Bridge last evening caused much surprise on account of the brilliant light that covered such a wide field."

The process had begun earlier that year in April, when H.H. Brown, esquire, petitioned the city to build a power plant in town. An ordinance was then filed in May 1887 by Salida's Board of Trustees approving Brown's request and stating the conditions for the plant to proceed.

The plan was to light sections of F Street, and some of the outlying streets, then followed by the Denver & Rio Grande railroad yards and the round house, the railroad depot, and the Monte Cristo Hotel.

In August, officers were elected to the board of the Edison Electric Light Company. Superintendent Robert M. Ridgway, who worked for the Denver & Rio Grande Railroad, was elected president.

By October, there was a large crew working on the plant on Sackett. A 75-foot smoke stack was installed and the electric lamps had arrived in town. The original 28 ft. square frame building had a boiler room, one 80 horsepower engine, and two incandescent dynamos, with a capacity for 750 incandescent lights.

The first building to have electric light in Salida was the Monte Cristo, the Denver & Rio Grande's hotel:

"The dining room of the Monte Cristo was brilliantly lighted up for the first time last Wednesday evening by electricity. 20 twenty-four candle power incandescent lamps were in use and gave the utmost satisfaction."

The Monte Cristo had one of the best restaurants in town and was a destination in Salida for either eating or for people watching as it was close to the Denver & Rio Grande depot. Writer Lacy Humbeutel remarked:

"Although the beautiful surroundings made dining a pleasure, it was the excellent food that attracted the crowds ... local people thronged to the Monte Cristo for midday, evening, and Sunday meals. All the men who worked at the two railroad turntables, the machine shop and other jobs in the yard ate at least one meal a day there."

In January 1888, the Edison Company suffered a small setback when fire swept through downtown. Peter Mulvany's hotel at 2nd & F caught fire, which spread in all four directions, a half a block each way. The town's total losses were valued at approximately $175,000. The electric plant came away with better fortune than most:

"The Electric Light Company is scorched but gives light at the usual time," though they did suffer a $500 loss from burned poles and wires.

Later that month, Denver & Rio Grande Superintendent and Edison Board President Ridgway had electric light in both his office and home. The D&RG had constructed several offices and buildings at the base of Tenderfoot Mountain and Ridgway may have lived and worked in the dwellings where the Junction House was located. Incidentally, Robert Ridgway later established the town of Ridgway in southwest Colorado.

By March, the light was pervasive and all of Salida's main streets were illuminated with Edison incandescent lamps:

"From darkness to torches, from torches to candles, from candles to oil lamps, from oil lamps to gas lighting, [these] were slow but sure steps in the evolution of artificial illumination. [W]hen Franklin snatched the lightning from the heavens he little dreamed that he was laying future generations under everlasting obligations to him as the author of the perfutim of artificial light."

In 1890, two new Edison dynamos were in use. By the end of that decade, a brick building replaced the wooden structure, which is what we see as the Steam Plant Theater today.

By the beginning of the 20th century, the Edison Company was suffering from mismanagement and in 1905, the shareholders had voted to sell out to Salida Light, Power, and Utility. The new company built two more plants; one dedicated to light, and one to power. In 1907, SLPU was repairing the original plant:

"When completed, those depending on the company for light and power need have no fear that some [day] they will be compelled to dig up old, rusty oil lamps or resticate 'Maud', the stubborn gas engine from the rubbish heap."

The Edison Electric Plant
at 220 W. Sackett

Seventeen

E.D. Cowen, Newspaperman

ED Cowen worked hard to get a good story. He hopscotched around the West working at various newspapers his entire life. He made a Grand Tour of Europe on his bicycle and wrote about it. He went to the Grand Canyon in search of John D. Lee, of Mountain Meadows massacre infamy, just for the interview. And he got the hell beat out of him in Leadville by one of the local bruisers, who exclaimed during the beating that Cowen "was the only newspaperman he had respect for."

He was something beyond a wordsmith, having an effortless command of the language, and he had a knack for telling a good story.

In 1880, Cowen was a managing editor at the Leadville Herald. That same year, when he was 23, he wrote a series of editorials, detailing the progress and mining work being done in the Monarch region. To that end, he took the Leadville stage heading south, and at Nathrop turned west towards Alpine, then looped back towards Monarch and Maysville. He was writing all the way.

The memorable trip from Leadville to Buena Vista allowed Cowen to sketch some of his fellow passengers on the stage from Leadville:

"The front seat was occupied by a don't-care element that comprised an expert going to Silver Cliff, a young blood who was tired of dissipation, a retired prospector with pockets well-lined, and three quart bottles nearly empty, [which were] going to be filled at the first station. A happy triplet. Didn't care whether they got in Buena Vista that night, or in a week. All the same. Life was short, full of woe. Might as well bury it in oblivion when we can. And thus, they viewed the situation among themselves."

From Buena Vista, his fellow travelers having disembarked, Cowen was the sole traveler in a stagecoach bouncing towards Alpine. The coach stopped at Hortense (today Mt. Princeton Hot Springs) to deliver the mail and Cowen spoke with the head of the Post Office, Major George Merriam. He declared the resort a popular location: "We have an abundance of the most curative of waters, an excellent climate, splendid scenery and plenty of it, good trout fishing, the best hunting ground, and a prospective railroad connection with the outside world. Is this not enough in itself?"

Cowen then headed towards Alpine, a town with two dance halls, a large colony, and a bad rap for having less than productive mines.

The Denver and Leadville newspaper editorialists dismissed Alpine as a "blasted hope" with no "mineral of consequence in the country" and as a result of this negative stereotyping, the Alpine denizens looked on newspaper reporters with a suspicious eye. Cowen attempted an olive branch, writing that Alpine has a "new and prosperous aspect...Everything about the place, from the mountains down has an air of solidity and permanence that is born of slow and studied growth." He didn't stay long. Next stop: Maysville.

In 1879, the site of Maysville was just ranch land owned by Amasa Feathers. By 1880, due to the success of the Monarch Mining Region, the town was platted and had a population of around 1,000. Cowen arrived to document the scene. Besides giving detailed descriptions of the mining activity in his editorial, Cowen gave the finer points of life in Maysville. The most notable instance of life in a small western town is the influence that alcohol has upon the local population. Here is Cowen describing a typical night for an inebriate in Maysville:

"An occasional insipid drunk is watched by the eagle-eyed marshal with an avidity that is amusing, and gloated over by the police judge with a delight that is almost fiendish. It's no use. A noisy worship at the shrine of Bacchus in Maysville is prolific of but one end, and that an unhappy one — the 'cooler' for the night, turbulent headache and untasted breakfast for the morning. At 10 a.m. the judge interrogates, the marshal witnesses and reiterates, the prisoner feels scanty purse and expostulates. It can't be helped, the court must execute its painful duty, and the victim of overindulgence is 'sherried' into the street. His pocketbook looks like a consumptive climbing Pike's Peak, and he leaves his personal effects in hock and hies to Poncha Springs or some other congenial clime."

At the time of Cowen's visit, John Hughes was the proprietor of the Hughes House in Maysville. His wife Nellie, demonstrated some serious spirit after four degenerates rolled into town wreaking havoc, mouthing off, and leaving saloons with unpaid bills. Cowen witnessed the melee and then wrote this anecdote:

"After a forenoon spent in this manner, they entered the Hughes Hotel, and in supercilious tones, called for dinner, supplemented by endless oaths. To this demand, Mrs. Hughes politely informed them that there was no dinner or hospitality in a house for such men, whereupon they sneered and laughed in a derisive manner, and redoubled their filthy language. The plucky little woman was immovable in her decision. The dining room was occupied by 27 male boarders eating dinner, of which fact the muscular quadrilateral was in ignorance, and when, after repeated assurances that they could not enter, they moved to a position in a closed doorway, with the evident intention of forcing their way, she threw the door open, and in an imperative voice demanded the assistance of the boarders. They responded to a man, and with the proverbial instinct of a coward cornered, they realized that they had the worst of it, and were not long in leaving the house."

Cowen wrote detailed descriptions of the Monarch Mining Region further west from Maysville. One notable history was of Nicholas Creede and his contributions to the area. Creede discovered the Great Monarch and Little Charm Mines but didn't see much in the way of valuable ore at either site, so he sold his claims to the Boon Brothers. The mines soon became rich producers and were sold for upwards of $60,000, and the new town that sprang up was named Monarch. There was no reason to pity Creede; he landed at Wagon Wheel Gap in the San Juans and discovered multiple mines, among them the famous Holy Moses vein. He also became namesake to the town of Creede.

The entire Monarch Mining Region was a bustling place in 1880, one with a bright future ahead of it. The miners working around the North Fork of the South Arkansas had transformed the area from a two-hut camp to "thirty substantial buildings...The present population as shown in the census returns is one hundred and ten people, most of whom are busily developing mining property in the vicinity."

The Shavano Band in the Monarch Mining Region, North Fork of the South Arkansas, 1880.

That Fourth of July was a merry one. Cowen finished up his tour at Maysville, and joined in the celebration. Races of all kinds were included in the lineup of the day: burro, wheelbarrow, sack, and foot, and every other type of outdoor amusement. It started with picnics and ended with dancing into the wee hours.

Cowen finished his epic piece with a nod to what all gold seekers in that day were coveting: a strike equal to that of Leadville:

"For the past few weeks there has been considerable talk of the district, but all the reports from it were construed as inflammatory, until last Saturday [three] well-known and reliable prospectors returned, laden with ores and brilliant prospects, coupled with the assertion that a second Leadville will be the ultimate result."

It was not to be. For sixty years, Lake County was the champion of Colorado in mineral wealth, having removed some $420 million from their hills. Chaffee County came in with significantly less, just $21 million.

Eighteen

Mineral Wealth in Chaffee County

The beauty of the mountains in Chaffee County have long held treasure: gold, silver, copper, marble and lime, along with gemstones in the rough, are just some of the glitter concealed in our locale. Some of these treasures have had interesting histories here and these are three of their stories.

Marble was discovered up near Monarch in 1883, and was of a good enough quality that a nationally-known mining journal took note:

"The marble discoveries on the northwest side of Monarch will be opened up for quarrying in a very short time. Such developments show this new and valuable property to be of great extent and the quality has been pronounced by experts to be very fine and beautiful."

This marble near Garfield rivaled "the noted Italian marble." It didn't take long before someone staked a claim:

"H.L. Acker has two claims in Taylor Gulch near Garfield in which the marble ledge is 2,000 feet long and from 150 to 200 feet wide. Mr. Acker proposes to put on a larger force of men and increase the output of the valuable quarry."

During the late 1880s, Denver had begun discussing the need to build a state capitol building. By the turn of the decade, excavation had begun in the mountains of Colorado to furnish this building material and roads were being built into the stone quarries. Much of the granite for the capitol would come from the Aberdeen Quarry in Gunnison. The marble that was to be used for the flooring would come from Marble, Colorado and also from Taylor Gulch, here in Chaffee County:

"D.J. Kelly, contractor for the marble work in the capitol building, will probably have 50 men at work in Taylor Gulch near Garfield, early in May, getting out white marble for the capitol building. Machinery will be put in and the marble tiling will be cut and dressed at the quarry. Mr. Kelly says Chaffee County has the finest white marble in the state."

That may have been a plug for Chaffee County commerce, but who knows? Our marble may have surpassed Marble's marble.

The Taylor Gulch ledge had been sufficiently depleted by 1910. The marble that remained was too coarse and was unsatisfactory for building.

—

In 1881, gem hunter Nelson Wanemaker staked a claim on Mount Antero, in search of aquamarines. Nelson would soon become the preeminent source for these blue-green stones. They were easily found in those early days, and Nelson was an avid hunter on the slopes of Antero. Reverend Roselle Cross, an early collector of Colorado gems, purchased many of Nelson's aquamarines. He was not alone: other Colorado geologists lined up, ready to buy from the champion gem hunter.

Besides aquamarines, Nelson also found other valuable pieces. In 1887, he fetched in a specimen of the lustrous green crystal called epidote. And he was the first person in the state of Colorado to discover corundum, a mineral which produces the gem varieties of ruby and sapphire.

Wanemaker aquamarines have since been distributed throughout the country. The American Museum of Natural History in New York and the Field Museum in Chicago are just two places where Wanemaker specimens are housed. Mineralogist Mark Jacobson wrote that if an aquamarine had a purchase date of between 1885 and 1893, "one can assume that it was collected by Wanemaker."

Besides selling to geologists and collectors, Nelson set up a stand at the Denver & Rio Grande rail depot and did a "good business at the trains selling specimens to the tenderfeet."

Today, the Krivanek claim in the Antero region is still productive. Krivanek Jewelers in downtown Salida has a nice display on hand of aquamarines in both rough and gem form.

—

Chaffee County was once considered the "granite center of the world." The granite found near Turret was equal to some of the best quarries in the world and the kings of the industry here were the Salida Granite Company:

"The Salida Granite Company is the oldest concern of its kind that has taken granite from the Turret district. Before locating their quarry, their president, Ed Bowen, in 1893, prospected the hills, and at that time there were no other granite claims. The consequence was that he picked a very fine ledge of granite that was accessible by means of the county road, known as the Ute Trail Road. So fine was the quality of this granite and so great the demand that a finishing plant was erected in Salida and wholesale as well as retail business was engaged in."

The Mining Science Journal from 1911 extolled upon the beauties of Salida granite:

"Its strength far exceeds that of most granites, while the beauty of its contrast cannot be equaled by any except perhaps Monticello, a mahogany colored jasper-like material quarried in Wisconsin, and which is the highest priced stone in the market today. The contrast between carved and polished surface is striking, the dressed surface showing very light, while the polished face is blue-black in color,

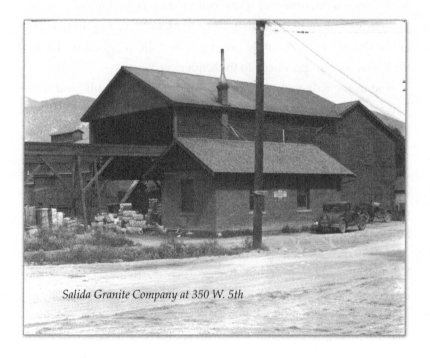

Salida Granite Company at 350 W. 5th

showing with great distinctness the lettering and other ornamentation."

Besides dark granite, Salida soon became famous for its rose-pink granite. American sculptors clamored for it. As a result, one can find Salida granite at many places around the nation. In several eastern U.S. cities, monuments to 16th century theologian Martin Luther are made of Salida granite. The memorial to Governor Frank Steunenberg in Idaho is built upon Salida granite. Most famously of all, the Mormon Battalion Monument in Salt Lake City was carved exclusively out of Salida rose-pink granite.

Cutting machinery inside the Salida Granite Company

By the mid-1930s, Salida's reputation as a granite producer was sealed. The Salida Granite Company was bringing in millions of dollars to the community. Even though it was a costlier granite, sculptors declared "there is no granite in the world that equals it because of the beautiful texture and the blending of the polished, hammered, and carved surfaces."

The quarries shut down in the 1970s but this carved granite can still be seen right here in Salida. Around 75% of the headstones in Fairview Cemetery are made of Salida granite. And the Salida Granite Company donated the cornerstone located at the northwest corner of the Salida Library.

Mormon Battalion Monument

Nineteen

The Poet of the Rockies

The label 'Poet of the Rockies' is a bold stamp to place upon any writer, and is one that some would not be able to live up to. It would take an education within the ranks of the Denver & Rio Grande Railroad before Cy Warman would be honored with this title.

Cy moved to Salida in 1885 and got a job with the Denver & Rio Grande Railroad, starting at ground level as a general laborer. Historian Nolie Mumey describes here what kind of work Cy was employed to do:

"On the second day of his new position, he was assigned to clean the ash pan of the 4-40, a twenty-ton locomotive with 45-inch drive wheels. The task of cleaning the pan required that he crawl under the hot engine and drag out the ashes with a hoe. The heat from the firebox was stifling, and the smoke and steam from the air pump were suffocating and blinding. The new recruit completed his task to the satisfaction of the foreman and the general manager who stood by watching the entire operation."

Cy was a dedicated employee and due to his hustle, it didn't take long for him to move up the ranks. Three months into his job, Cy was promoted to fireman aboard the D&RG locomotives. It was a step up because he was riding in the engine, but still, it was backbreaking work shoveling coal into the great steam engines. Writer Samuel Dougherty describes a typical day:

"The job of fireman in those days was more than going for a ride on a swaying, pounding, jolting locomotive; more than hard, physical labor shoveling 20 tons of coal in the firebox during a 16-hour tour of duty. It wasn't just shaking grates, bogging ash pans, and eating smoke and cinders in the heat and dust. It was a way of life that extended beyond the hours in the cab."

After a few years, Cy reached the pinnacle for a railroadman: Locomotive Engineer. This is when Cy began to earn his title of 'Poet of the Rockies.' His runs included Salida to Gunnison (via Marshall Pass) and Salida up to Leadville. Later on, Cy would observe: "I couldn't help writing poetry with such scenery as that to run my engine through" and that was the beginning of Cy's writing career.

Here is one of Cy's poems, an ode to what is known today as Big Horn Sheep Canyon and the Royal Gorge:

The Canon of the Grand

I'm going to paint a picture with a pencil of my own;
I shall have no hand to help me; I shall paint it all alone.
Oft I fancy it before me, and my hopeful heart grows faint,
As I contemplate the grandeur of the picture I would paint.

When I rhyme about the river, the laughing, limpid stream,
Whose ripples seem to shiver, as they glide and glow and gleam;
Of the waves that beat the boulders that are strewn upon the strand,
You will recognize the river in the Canon of the Grand.

When I write about the mountains, with their heads so high and hoar,
Of the cliffs and craggy canons, where the waters rush and roar;
When I speak about the walls that rise so high on either hand,
You will recognize the rockwork in the Canon of the Grand.

God was good to make the mountains, the valleys and the hills,
Put the rose upon the cactus and the ripple on the rills;
But if I had all the words of all the worlds at my command,
I could not paint a picture of the Canon of the Grand.

Cy was also influenced by the excitement and dangers of railroading. He wrote many railroad tales, many of which documented true-life cases of desperate circumstances on the line. Nolie Mumey describes one instance of the treacherous conditions: "The track over Marshall Pass went up to an altitude of 10,000 feet, with 4% grades and 24 degree curves. [Cy] was in many snow battles – one lasted eight days, where he bucked snowdrifts and spent forty consecutive hours in the cab without any rest. It was a tough run."

Cy ran the Calumet Branch line only once. This was a notorious line that spurred off from the main D&RG line to Leadville, turning at Hecla Junction and going straight up to the Colorado Fuel and Iron Company's mine. It was seven miles with a 7% grade. A locomotive engine pushed up empty cars but could only bring down four loaded cars. That was all the engine brakes could handle. Cy Warman called it 'The Perpendicular Railroad' and he wrote a story about it, which was later published in his volume *Short Rails*.

Cy was forced to retire from the railroad due to sciatic rheumatism, and in 1888 he started his own newspaper in Salida. He named it *The Frog*, railroad terminology for the split where two rail

lines cross. It was dedicated to railroading tales and news, but was soon bought out and renamed *Western Railway* magazine. From there, Cy began to ramble around the state in search of new writing jobs.

In 1891, Cy got a job writing for the *Rocky Mountain News* where he worked for a short while, and then he wound up in Creede, where he started up another newspaper, this one the *Creede Chronicle*. It was another short-lived enterprise that lasted around 6 months, only because Cy had stiff competition from the other Creede newspapers. But while he was there, Cy wrote one of his most memorable poems:

Creede

Here's a land where all are equal –
Of high or lowly birth –
A land where men make millions,
Dug from the dreary earth.
Here the meek and mild-eyed burro
On mineral mountains feed –
It's day all day, in the day-time,
And there is no night in Creede.

The cliffs are solid silver,
With wond'rous wealth untold,
And the beds of running rivers
Are lined with glittering gold.
While the world is filled with sorrow,
And hearts must break and bleed –
It's day all day, in the day-time,
And there is no night in Creede.

Following the newspaper bust in Creede, Cy began his writing career in earnest, selling his pieces out to many different publications. He also published several books of his poetry and short stories. One of his poems, 'Sweet Marie,' was set to music and became a popular hit of the era. It was featured in the 1947 film *Life with Father*.

When Cy was 56 years old, he published a book of poems entitled *Songs of Cy Warman*. One had a brush of foreshadowing:

Will the Lights Be White?

Oft, when I feel my engine swerve,
As o'er strange rails we fare,

I strain my eye around the curve
For what awaits us there.
When swift and free she carries me
Through yards unknown at night,
I look along the line to see
That all the lamps are white.

The blue light marks the crippled car,
The green light signals slow;
The red light is a danger light,
The white light, "Let her go."
Again the open fields we roam,
And, when the night is fair,
I look up in the starry dome
And wonder what's up there.

For who can speak for those who dwell
Behind the curving sky?
No man has ever lived to tell
Just what it means to die.
Swift toward life's terminal I trend,
The run seems short tonight;
God only knows what's at the end –
I hope the lamps are white.

Cy died three years later.

Twenty

Being Black in Salida

In the post-Civil War era, many Black Americans migrated out of the South, away from an enslaved past. They headed north and west, and some landed in Colorado. Salida's Black American population was largely hidden from view. From a historical perspective their voices were concealed, and their image was distorted through a white lens.

At the time, one job opportunity that was available to Black American men was that of railroad porter. The Pullman porters were a presence on the Denver & Rio Grande rails system here in Salida and the Pullman Company exclusively hired Black American men to be porters, a move George Pullman made purposefully. Porters were to be seen as subservient to the white train traveler, a throwback to enslaved times.

Poor wages, long working conditions (400 hours a month), and no room for advancement made a porter's life bleak. Porters learned early on how to supplement their wages with tips.

Malcolm X, who was a railroad porter prior to becoming the voice of a generation, described the strange interplay that came with the job:

"It didn't take me a week to learn that all you had to do was give white people a show and they'd buy anything you offered them. The dining car waiters and Pullman porters knew it too, and they faked their Uncle Tomming to get bigger tips. We were in that world of Negroes who are both servants and psychologists, aware that white people are so obsessed with their own importance that they will pay liberally, even dearly, for the impression of being catered to and entertained."

Along with these porters, there were Black Americans working as shopkeepers, menial laborers, and prostitutes in town. Isolated away from F Street, the designated area for the "Negro tenements" was on G Street, near the D&RG narrow gauge railroad tracks between Sackett and First streets. There they were invisible.

On the occasion that Black people were featured in the local paper, it was usually due to disorderly conduct. They provided sensationalism in a predominantly white community, and the newspaper made it a practice to paint Blacks as deviants. That Black Americans were an integral part of the workings of the Denver & Rio Grande railroad was beside the point. Newspapers would intentionally run negative articles when they reported on Black American activities in the community.

To illustrate this point, the Salida Mail's report of a crime committed against a prostitute in downtown Salida was rife with prejudice:

"A good share of the colored population were under arrest last Wednesday in order to ascertain the assailant of one 'Lucille' of the demimonde. The dusky maiden was attacked with a hatchet and one of her eyes nearly chopped out and then left in the alley to bleed to death. She was picked up by the authorities at night and every suspicious Negro in town was put under arrest, there being nearly fully 25 within the city jail at present."

This racial profiling made it a sure thing that Blacks would be included in any roundup. What followed was a forced relocation at the turn of the 20th century:

"Mayor Dupar and the police determined to stop the nuisance and in order to do so resolved that the colored tenderloin element must go. The work of clearing the lower quarters of the city of this element has been going on for some time ... Now there is not a single one of the dusky females left in the district and consequent to their removal their worthless and degenerate colored paramours have also mostly disappeared, for they lived from the funds supplied them by the women."

One of the racist tactics employed then used language equating a Black person with vermin: "There are two or three other 'nests' that are spotted and will soon be cleaned out. The determination is to rid the city of this scum that has been allowed to collect and pollute the social atmosphere." Proof of Black skin was disparaged by the population at large.

The local paper admitted the disparities, headlining an article entitled "Black Man's Burden Greater in Salida" and proposing that "...All members of the race who are minus the visible means of support will be compelled to skiddoo within the next ten days or two weeks. Salida people have not as yet decided to allow the man of color to go as he pleases or do as he pleases."

Besides the porters and prostitutes, there were Black Americans who didn't live in Salida but came to town to work in minstrel shows.

The 19th century minstrel show may have started as a novelty for whites, but it eventually devolved into a significant racial stereotype that permeated the definition of what it was to be Black in America. These popular shows toured America in force in the early 20th century. American theatres catered to the cravings of audiences to see

Minstrel band coming into Salida

whites portraying Blacks.

A sampling of advertisements from this time period declared the attractions: the "Young family, in their big, black, laughing pantomime," and Oliver Scott's minstrel carnival with its "really funny coons."

When Black Americans were in the tour production, they were assigned the role of musician, or minstrel. White actors blackened their faces and portrayed the part of Black Americans.

Even here in Salida a recipe for 'burnt cork' was printed in the newspaper so local actors could star in their own minstrel shows. The local Elks chapter staged their own production in 1907. The burnt cork recipe was helpful to them:

Band in downtown Salida

"Prominent business men, whom you see on the streets every day, will sing, joke, tell stories and dance with the grace and abandon of old-time professionals" and they completed their caricatures with darkened faces. To expand on the joke, the paper published racist cartoon images; the captions they added included the names of prominent Elks club members.

Salida, Colo., Dec. 2, 1908.

Carnagie Library Board,
    Salida, Colo.
        I, the undersigned, do hereby make application to
your Honorable Body as Janiter for Library Building.
        Can furnish good references.
                        Respectfully,

                                    Henry Stroup.
                            Colored.

J. N. Randol

J. E. Cook,

Paul Stoolff

Louis Bonhajo

Mrs. H. F. Bullard

*Henry Stroup applied to the library for the custodian position in 1908.
The word 'colored' is stamped after his signature.*

Reports of positive news were few and far between. Church announcements were one example. This was in keeping with trends around the country, as the only information that pertained to Black Americans that was recorded in the local city directories was church-related. In 1909, a local missionary group requested funding for a 'colored church.' A short time later, the A.M.E. (African Methodist Episcopal) Mission Church was holding services at the Watson Chapel and their advertisement in the newspaper read: "All are welcome to these services." The 1909 Salida city directory does in fact list the Watson Chapel as a place of worship.

One favorable item and rare occurrence that was reported was this bit of good being committed by a Black man, who cleared the D&RG tracks after they were covered in mud and debris from a flash flood. The local newspaper referred to him as a 'friend' and then reported his name: 'William Boyer, colored.'

These small items of what life was like for Black Americans is just a small representation. The larger history is lost to time because of racist attitudes. The writer James Baldwin observed that "People are not … terribly anxious to be equal (equal, after all, to what and to whom?) but they love the idea of being superior. And this human truth has an especially grinding force here, where identity is almost impossible to achieve and people are perpetually attempting to find their feet on the shifting sands of status."

Twenty-One

Salida's Wheelmen

The relationship between America's youth and the bicycle began in earnest in the 1880s. Until then, bicycles had been expensive, cumbersome, and dangerous affairs with names like 'Boneshaker' but with the advent of the safety bicycle, which was cheaper to manufacture and resembles what we ride today, the bicycle finally became available to the working classes. By today's standards, these bikes were primitive.

In 1883, a couple of members from a bicycle club in Missouri were kicked out of class for wearing scandalous knee breeches to school. In retaliation against the school, the Club signed an agreement which stated to the effect that knee breeches were superior to long pants and that they would adopt them as customary wear at all times for an entire year:

"Twelve members of the club signed the petition in defiance of the social order. Their teacher told them that they would be required to remain at home until they were willing to appear in the classroom attired like other male pupils. This action made the teacher very unpopular among the wheelmen, and a few girls, who admired the 'sawed off pants.'"

The bicycle moved west. Salida had one lone bicycle owner in 1884. By 1888, a club was in its infancy in Salida: "Salida will have a bicycle club as soon as the Poncha Boulevard is complete." The Eddy Bros. addition on the mesa just west of Salida, ensured that the club would have a decent roadway to ride on: "The Poncha Boulevard will soon be an attractive resort for owners of 'flyers' and for the young men and their best girls when out for a drive on Sunday afternoons."

City Council soon responded to requests from local cyclists and Poncha Boulevard was graded down, the road being set out 100 feet wide to a distance of five miles, all the way to Poncha Springs. It was made amenable for both cyclists and horse-drawn buggies.

In April of 1891, things were rolling along with the Salida Bicycle Club and they began to schedule bike outings. On one Sunday morning they "went up to Buena Vista on the accommodation [the Salida to Leadville train] and rode back on their wheels. They started from Buena Vista at 1 p.m. and arrived here in Salida at 6 p.m., a distance of something over 30 miles by the wagon road."

By the following month, local stores were selling "bike suits" and it can be presumed that some of these included knee breeches, just like what the boys in Missouri were wearing who were kicked out of class. The month after that, City Council was issuing ordinances which made it a misdemeanor to run your bicycle or tricycle on the sidewalks. Offenders were fined not less than $10 but not more than $50.

By 1892 there was an offshoot club, the Monarch Bicycle Club, which was making runs up to the top of the pass and back, a brutal climb at high elevation "eclipsing all former records. [Members felt] confident that they can compete successfully with any club in the county, or state."

With all these bicycles in town and the outer regions, it was inevitable that the kids would start racing each other.

The first instance of bike racing occurred here in September 1892 between Ed Krueger of Buena Vista and Walter Bateman (one of the Bateman Hardware kids) of Salida. The race course had a start at Buena Vista and ended just below the Nathrop red school house. Unfortunately for Salida fans, Bateman lost the race and an $80 purse. It turns out, there was some controversy during the race:

"It must be said in all fairness to the statement made by Bateman, which is universally believed, and Krueger's story being to the contrary, that Krueger did not win the race fairly. Bateman met with an accident [and] nothing short of a severe tumble or being knocked clear out of the road could result so disastrously. Bateman's pedal was bent so that it would not revolve and besides he, in falling, bruised and skinned his leg and knee in a horrible shape. No ordinary fall could do this. Bateman says Krueger fouled him. Krueger says Bateman fouled him. Anybody that knows Walter Bateman knows he would not foul a person under any circumstances, nor would he lie about it."

The previous was written by Salida's local paper, so bias is certainly involved, but perhaps this is what initiated the sports rivalry between Buena Vista and Salida.

Another bike club was organized in April 1894 after "a number of Salida's devotees of the wheel had enjoyed a pleasant run among the mountain roads ... Those who have inaugurated this movement hope to augment the club until its membership will number every wheelman in the city. Another meeting will take place next Sunday and a run will leave the city at 9 a.m. Every wheelman in town is invited to participate." This announcement ended with a directive to potential bike club members -- 'No Scorching.'

On a Sunday May morning in 1894, six members of the Bike Club rode the unpaved roads from Salida to Saguache. Of the six, two of the riders dug deep and completed the round trip in 8 ½ hours. One of those two just happened to be Walter Bateman.

Not to be outdone, the ladies of Salida had begun purchasing bicycles and "the subject of organizing a ladies' wheel club is being agitated."

Having a set of wheels meant having freedom and for women, these were the first steps towards emancipation, although some women of the era were not fully supportive. The French film actor Sarah Bernhardt was quoted: "I look out of my coupe in the park and I see women in bloomers, Very strange! Everybody rides – men, women, children. Bloomers? Oh no! Women of good family and position do not wear them, although the best women, the grand dames, ride bicycles."

Later that May, it was announced "All cyclists, whether members of the Salida Wheel Club or not, are invited to meet at the corner of F and 5th Streets at 9 a.m. on Wednesday, May 30, for a run around the circle on the mesa. The ladies are especially invited to be present and participate in the run. The pace will be set by the slowest rider and the run will be under the direction of Captain Walter Bateman and Lieutenant Arthur Hawthorne." The kids were using bicycling as a way to hook up.

This announcement was the first mention of the Salida Wheel Club, which was probably an amalgamation of all the other clubs into one, though the Ladies Club and eventually, the Juvenile Club would remain separate and distinct.

The first big bike race in Salida was organized in August of 1895. The course started at Salida's F and 3rd Street crossing, went up the mesa to Poncha Boulevard, and ended at the top of Piñon Canon (above the Poncha Depot) where the racers would turn and come back into Salida, a round trip distance of 12 miles. Of the eleven that entered, only six started, and four ultimately finished. The race was rife with cheating, with racers being accused of dismounting and carrying bikes, cutting off at bends in the road, and one racer who was paced by a fresh rider from Poncha Springs. The judges conferred and after deliberation disqualified the offending racers. The prizes were no doubt the reason for the cheating:

"The first time prize gold medal for the road race ... was purchased at a cost of $15 and is a very handsome affair. It is of solid 14 karat gold, and the design is a bicycle in relief resting upon a crescent shaped base upon which is engraved FIRST TIME PRIZE. On the back are the words 12 MILE ROAD RACE, AUGUST 15, 1895. In the bar is inscribed SALIDA WHEEL CLUB. The second time prize, a solid silver medal is a very handsome and substantial piece of work. It consists of a shield-shaped pendant and bar, mounted on a fine silk ribbon. The words engraved are substantially the same as those on the gold medal and on the pendant is engraved a bicycle."

The following paragraph ran in the Salida Mail newspaper on April 22, 1890:

"J.N. Simmons is fond of bicycle riding – very. He was out for a ride yesterday afternoon when the wheel struck an obstacle and Mr. Simmons took a header. He received some slight bruises and the bicycle has been sent to the shop for repairs."

By 1896, Salida was officially a bike town: "The number of bicycles in Salida is somewhat surprising and the fever still grows."

That year's Decoration Day Bike Race was the talk of the town. The race course was set the same as the previous year, from F Street, up Poncha Boulevard to Poncha Springs, and then back to Salida, a round trip distance of 12 miles. Just like the previous year's race, the winners prizes were very swanky: "The bar [on the First Time Prize] represents the handle bars of a bicycle entwined with ribbons on which will be engraved the date and the time of the winner and the pendant is crescent-shaped with a small gold bicycle wheel in the center – the wheel having an enamel tire and three gold rings about the hub. Around the crescent is a laurel wreath of gold tied at the bottom by a gold ribbon. Hanging from the bar is a small gold bicycle lamp. Two genuine garnets are set, one in the center of the hub and the other in the lantern. The second time prize is a silver medal very much on the plan of the gold one and is as pretty a creation in silver as could well be gotten up. Instead of the garnets, diamonds are set in the lantern and in the wheel hub."

The big day included a bike parade and "every man, woman, and child who can beg, borrow, buy, or swipe a wheel is expected to take part in this parade. The more elaborately decorated the wheel the better. If you can't ride, get someone to hold the wheel up and push you."

Twenty-two riders signed up for the race; over half were from out of town. The Salida Band was musically omnipresent, playing throughout the race, and then again during the parade. The day of the race, the Salida Mail gave full commentary:

"Everyone made a good start and they were eagerly watched far up the mesa road by the large crowd of spectators assembled to see them. As soon as the last man was well on his way the crowd moved to the place of the finish at the crossing of F and 4th streets. For a distance of three blocks, the spectators crowded the walks, sat on the fences and even stood in the ditches, so eager were they to witness the finish. Soon after, the first rider appeared flying down the street. Everybody held their breath for a moment and then a big cheer went up from the crowd when it was seen that a Salida boy was first over the line and would carry off the big prize. Densmore [the winner] came in as fresh as if he had ridden only a mile and with a smile on his face as much as to say, 'How astonishingly easy.'" William

Densmore won the race in 42 minutes 39 seconds and along with his gold medal, valued at $50, he received a pair of $15 Morgan & Wright tires.

Bike brands were important. It was noted what the racers were riding: "York rode a Temple Scorcher, Densmore a Hamilton, and Gilbert a Victor."

After the race was over, "the Grand Parade of Wheelmen was formed at Alpine Park. First came the Ladies' Cycling Club, followed by two junior organizations. All were uniformed and to say that they presented a beautiful appearance but faintly expresses the impression made upon the great crowd of spectators. The universal opinion was that the ladies were charming, the girls too cute for anything, and the little tots simply too sweet. Following were the local and visiting gentlemen, making in all 100 riders in line. It was quite a novel as well as pretty sight and carried its own impression of the strength of the wheelmen's forces."

For some years, Salida's wheelmen had been attempting to set up a bike relay race between Salida and Denver. In June of 1897, it all came together. The participants included members from the Salida club, as well as clubs from Canon City, Colorado Springs, and Denver.

Salida was the starting point and contributed twelve riders to the race. Participants switched off every five miles and then a fresh relay rider would begin, each one passing a satchel bag as they traversed the route. It was 216 miles to Denver and the race started early, at 4 a.m.

The last relay rider reached Denver at 7 p.m that night, which calculated out to the riders averaging 15 miles an hour during the race:

"This remarkable feat was accomplished by dividing the distance into short relays and covering it at the utmost speed to be got out of wheels and legs under all kinds of conditions. Considering that the roads were almost uniformly bad – mountainous in some places, muddy in others and rough for the rest – the time made was excellent."

There was a message in that satchel bag that was received by the Denver mayor. It was an invitation from Salida's mayor to all Denver citizens: "We extend to you and your people a most cordial invitation to come and assist us in celebrating the glorious Fourth of July."

Besides engaging in racing and long distance rides around Salida, the Wheelmen were considering building a bike track for their members. On August 5, 1896, the Salida Athletic Association was formed at one of the wheelmen's meetings. Members of the association went scouting to find a suitable location for a bike track. The site for a three-lap dirt track was located near the Arkansas River at the back of the property of the Electric Light Company (today the Steam Plant.) The Wheelmen estimated that the cost of the track, including fencing and seating, would be $750. To help raise money, the Salida Athletic Association worked with the Ladies' Cycling Club and set up a benefit ball for the building of the track. They succeeded in their fundraising and the track was in use by July 1897. But this was no indoor velodrome. Due to maintenance difficulties, the track was soon abandoned. Football games were later held at the site.

In 1897, the Wheelmen's club was reorganized and a new division was implemented:

"Wheelmen's organizations have ceased to be merely a matter of ornament and have become an instrument of actual utility in the affairs of a city or town that is well-nigh indispensable. Recognizing this fact, the wheelmen of the Salida Club have organized a wheel division, the object of which is to promote the art of wheeling, and to promote the improvements of the road. The requirement of membership in the Salida Club is the ability to ride a wheel. The division colors are cardinal red and royal purple and a uniform will be adopted later. Club runs will be called once a week by the captain."

It was the golden age of cycling, though it didn't last. Automobiles eventually replaced bicycles but there is no doubt that early Salida was the epitome of a bike town. Then, as now, "Bicycles are in as common use in January as in June. In fact, our little valley has a climate peculiar to itself which is unexcelled for pure excellence in the whole of the United States."

Twenty-Two

Vigilante Justice

In January of 1891, Hollis D. Spencer got a job as a police officer for the city of Salida, with a starting salary of $90 per month. Less than two months later, Hollis would be witness to one of the worst instances of mob justice in the town's history.

In Salida's early days, the Denver & Rio Grande was a major employer in town. They made up the fabric of Salida and everyone either worked for the railroad or catered to them. Back then, the Denver & Rio Grande steam trains were powered by coal and occasionally, D&RG firemen who were hasty in their work would accidentally shovel coal over the side of the engines. In a charitable act, the Denver & Rio Grande gave the poorer citizens of Salida the opportunity to pick up any dropped coal in the Salida rail yards. Many of these less fortunate citizens were of Italian descent. The local paper referred to them as 'dagos,' a slur meaning 'Diego,' directed towards people of Italian or Spanish descent.

On a Saturday afternoon in February 1891, D&RG employee Oliver Briley was working at the coal chutes in the rail yards when he got into an altercation with a group of Salida's Italian citizens who were taking refuse coal from the rail yard. The Italians overtook Briley in the brawl, bloodying and bruising him up. From that point on, Briley carried a gun. One week later, an Italian was gathering refuse coal in the yards when he elicited the ire of Briley. Briley drew his gun and ordered the man to drop the coal.

P.J. Sullivan, a popular D&RG conductor, saw what was going on:

"Sullivan … had witnessed Briley's affair with the dago, and … told Briley in a very kindly way that he ought not to draw a gun on a dago and prevent him from taking the coal, as the dagos had always been permitted to take the waste coal; that they had done so before Briley came and probably would long after Briley was gone. Briley took offense at this and said, 'Perhaps you would like to take it up. Perhaps you want something of me.' Sullivan replied that he guessed he could take anything Briley could give him, at which he got up and took off his overcoat. At the same time, Briley took off his overcoat and started down from the engine. As Sullivan advanced he picked up a piece of fence board about two feet long with which he made a pass at Briley. The latter warded the blow off with his left hand and with his right he reached for his revolver, which he carried … under his right vest pocket. As soon as Briley drew his revolver, he held it to Sullivan's abdomen and fired."

P.J. Sullivan was mortally wounded and died a short time later at the Denver & Rio Grande Hospital. Salida's marshal soon placed Briley under arrest in front of the Saddle Rock Restaurant, at 131 Lower F.

Earlier in the year, the town jail had burned to the ground, so for the time being prisoners were kept temporarily in a back room at the New England Dining Parlor, which was located at 117 W. 2nd.

Oliver Briley was leg-chained to the floor in the back of the parlor and sat in wait. Meanwhile, news spread like wildfire through town of the deed he had committed and 'whispers of lynching were heard.'

As a precaution, Marshal McKelvey swore in six additional deputies to reinforce his roster of three (Hollis Spencer included) and they took up their positions, well-armed, at the makeshift jail. Briley's brother secured a Winchester rifle and joined the deputies.

About 9 o'clock in the evening, a mob gathered in the streets of Salida. Masked men carrying rope proceeded towards the jail and lay siege to it. The mob broke the door in but when the deputies fired shots at them, they dispersed.

A couple of hours later, another attack was made on the jail. This time numerous shots were fired on both sides. The mob moved to the rear of the jail, continuing to volley bullets at the officers. Multiple people were injured, including Hollis Spencer who was standing in the front door with a revolver in each hand. The bullet that struck him 'creased his head' and he staggered back.

With bullets zinging, and the crowd seething, the officers were finally overpowered and the mob broke through, into the jail where Briley stood chained:

"The mob placed a rope around the prisoner's neck and dragged him out of the building. They made an attempt to hang him to the cross-beam of an electric light pole nearby, but the rope was not long enough. The prisoner's neck was broken and he was dead [by this] time."

The crowd had done their deed but were still vengeful: "[Oliver Briley's] brother came up and asked for the corpse. Some of the crowd were disposed to let him have it; others said no, and [the corpse] was accordingly taken to the railroad crossing sign at the point where First Street crosses the railroad and there he was strung up and left."

It was mob justice doled out in the streets of Salida.

Hollis Spencer

Later that evening, Sheriff Crymble (who had been in Buena Vista at the time) organized a coroner's jury and they cut Briley's body down at around 1 a.m. His body had been shot full of holes.

Hollis Spencer had stayed with the body until the Sheriff assembled his men and his night was later recalled:

"A group of lynchers, 15 in number, [were] very angry because of [Spencer] protecting the dead boy, and instructed him 'to wade the Arkansas,' an expression used then meaning to leave town and never return, or else. Undaunted, he took a position behind the old 'iron mike' at the corner of First and [G] Streets, unlimbered two 45s, and dared his enemies, across the street, to come and get him. The lynchers, sensing the apparent disastrous result of such a venture, wisely left the vicinity."

Some of the vigilantes were later identified and arrested, but every case against them was dismissed. In later years a retrospective was written: "Most of those closely associated with the tragedy and its victims have moved away or are dead. The memory is all that is left and the curse it left for so long seems to have faded away."

Twenty-Three

Disorderly Salida

When the Denver & Rio Grande Railroad established Salida in 1880, businesses soon followed in order to service the rail workers. Behind them came the disorderly houses: these were the gambling dens, brothels, saloons, and opium dens. Laura Evans (or Evens) was the biggest player in town; as a brothel owner, she commanded a large section of West Front Street (now Sackett Street), which became a line of demarcation in Salida.

Every night, but especially on the weekends, Front Street was a cacophony of loud music, drunken patrons, hustlers, and whores. FIBArk's got nothing on Front Street in Salida in 1900. Miners, who earned on average $150 to $200 a month, were regulars in the Red Light District. Meanwhile, the Denver & Rio Grande was shuttling in out-of-towners every day and they turned downtown into a festival every night.

By the early 1900s, the sex trade and the vices that go along with it was booming in Salida. Laura remembers how she got into the business:

"I didn't know anything about this business in Denver [around the 1890s] but I fell very readily into it … you don't know what to do, the money's so fast and everything … Paydays [a girl could] make a couple hundred [dollars]. You just helped yourself to what they had. You let a miner go back up the mountain with any money, they'd think you were crazy. I remember having men throw a fifty in your lap. And maybe you'd get 'em so full they couldn't see straight."

Laura's statement can be illustrated in the following anecdote, told memorably by the Salida Mail in January of 1897:

"Christiansen Bjornson arrived in Salida from Lake City Monday night and immediately proceeded to gaze with such fondness on the bad whisky…that he soon lost all count of himself and, not having a guardian to keep cases on his erratic movements, [he] naturally wandered into the Tenderloin district. He remained in the district and saloons for the greater part of two days when he came to the conclusion that he had been held up, as it were, for the sum of about $200."

The police were called in to investigate and "about all that Bjornson can say for certain is that he came to town and that now he is broke … He was seen during the two days and nights spending and giving away money with a free and lavish hand, which is probably the correct explanation for his present predicament."

No evidence could be found of theft so the case was dropped.

Between 1911 and 1913, there were 630 arrests for drunkenness and 443 for prostitution. At least three prostitutes attempted suicide in 1913; two were successful. Townsfolk finally wearied of all the vice and squalor and it roiled to a head that year. Salida's 'Morals Committee' began to agitate to clean up Salida. During this time there were many community meetings in an attempt to come up with solutions. Town leaders and citizens discussed at length the pros and cons of the Red-light District.

Some community members were against the closing of the District, arguing that smelter workers and Denver & Rio Grande employees were frequent patrons and removing brothels could have negative consequences; namely, that men with uncontrollable impulses would resort to rape if they didn't have the brothel outlet, weakly arguing that sexual violence can be equated with sexual gratification.

Most citizens were for cleaning up downtown and as a start, Salida moved away from its ordinance of fining local prostitutes. The city was in the habit of gathering 'monthly stipulations' from prostitutes. Mayor Alexander spoke about this: "This system has been distasteful to everyone, as it has the effect of placing the city in partnership with the Red Light District."

In June of 1913, Salida officials, the Morals Committee, and Laura Evans all conferred together and a plan was established to remove Salida's Red-light District.

By July, most of the smaller Front Street resorts were closed. The plan was gradual; Laura's large parlor house at 129 W. Sackett was set to close the following year. But Laura kept her business running until the mid-1940s, though it never saw the hey-day of the early years again.

Closing down the Red-light District was the first step in cleaning up downtown; the State of Colorado took care of Salida's drinking problem when prohibition was enacted.

Colorado went dry beginning January 1st, 1916. Prohibition seemed to work: three months after its enactment, the Chaffee County jail was without prisoners for the first time in years, "showing that the criminal element that follows the saloon is gradually leaving for more agreeable territory." In 1916, sixty-three people were arrested for drunk and disorderly conduct as compared to 249 in 1915.

The only way to get liquor (besides bootlegged) was through a specially-licensed pharmacist. Prescriptions were required for booze, so the obvious next step was to make your own.

In 1922, Mike Calvano's still at his Front Street house blew up, and in an effort to evade the law, he grabbed the still and took off towards the Arkansas River. Before he got there, the Marshal nabbed him. Mike pleaded: "Marshal, if you let me drop this still in the river, I will do whatever you say." The Marshal was unconvinced and Mike and his still appeared in court the next day where he was fined $50.

After prohibition was enacted, every bar in town had an open door policy, inviting skeptics in to check for stills or other illicit activities. Nothing to see here, the bars only sold soft drinks. To bypass the law, bootleggers in downtown Salida probably used the shared basements between buildings and the outdoor stairwells that were accessible to the basements of these buildings.

Stealth and a little luck was needed to buy and sell illegal hooch. Unfortunately for Frank Filippone, his luck ran out when he came clinking out of the Palace Hotel. Upon his arrest, officers found 29 pints of booze in his possession.

Twenty-Four

The Innkeeper & The Ambassador

In 1883, the Denver & Rio Grande Railroad built the Monte Cristo Hotel, just across the F Street Bridge. At a cost of $38,000, it was also a railroad dining establishment, set up to take care of hungry travelers on stopover. The D&RG Depot was located just next door, making it a prime location.

Charles Catlin moved to Salida in 1899 and took over management of the Monte Cristo. It was a fortuitous decision because along with the hotel, Charles inherited the dog that came with it.

Charles was good at his job; immediately it became clear that Salida's social scene was now happening at the Monte Cristo. Dinners were luxurious affairs; one particular Easter supper included oysters on the half shell, leg of spring lamb with mint sauce, and pineapple ice cream.

Besides fine dining, parties and whist games were popular diversions held at the Monte Cristo. One November evening in 1903, Charles and his wife hosted a stereopticon party for 150 people at the hotel, an 'illustrated lecture' of the Chicago World's Fair. It concluded with a social hour of refreshments and musical entertainment from a three-piece mandolin orchestra.

When trains ran hectic and the depot was busy, Charles kept his cool, handling the influx of travelers with a deft hand. Huge crowds coming in on the trains precipitated the need for emergency (and creative) dining outside of the Monte Cristo:

"On Wednesday, there were two sections of No. 5 and three of No. 1, all large trains and each coach crowded. The depot scene here each day is a lively and interesting one. Many of the trains have no diner and Manager Catlin of the Monte Cristo has arranged eating and refreshment quarters in front of the hotel, where business is transacted in a lively manner from ten to twenty minutes after each train pulls in."

But the biggest attraction at the Monte Cristo, and the greatest ambassador Salida ever had, was Duke (also known as Buster), the 8-year-old water spaniel who Charles inherited when he assumed management of the hotel. Duke was special:

"Everyone knew him and spoke to him as he passed up and down the streets; everybody was his friend. He was a faithful favorite among the commercial traveling men who then made Salida. He was in evidence upon the arrival of all trains and knew all the regular guests of the hotel as they alighted from the trains and greeted them with a smile of recognition."

Duke died in 1902, and Charles placed his body, bedecked with flowers, in a small coffin. The Monte Cristo staff and guests, and the

The Monte Cristo Hotel

Denver & Rio Grande railroad workers all formed a procession and carried Duke up to his final resting place on Tenderfoot Mountain.

When a Denver newspaperman, who was a frequent traveler to Salida, found out this news, he wrote the following:

"We got back in time to sit round the Monte Cristo hotel for an hour or two waiting for No. 4. The place didn't seem quite natural, and for some time we couldn't understand why, but suddenly it popped into our minds that Buster was not attending to duty.

"'What has become of Buster?' we asked.

"'He is dead and buried up there on Tenderfoot Hill.'

"The news shocked us. Buster knew everybody around Salida and counted everybody his friend. He had a way of introducing himself to strangers. We will never forget the first time we met him. He stepped in front of us and surveyed us carefully from head to foot, then he wagged his tail and barked an introduction. We held out our hand and he came to us and rubbed his healthy, moist nose alongside of our face. That was enough, we were friends."

A few months after Duke died, Charles built a trail up to his grave and placed a wooden monument there. He framed Duke's obituary and his photograph and placed it at the tomb. The following words were inscribed:

In Memory of Duke
A Faithful Dog
of the Monte Cristo Hotel
Died October 29, 1902

With that, a legend was born, and the pilgrimage to Duke's grave became one of the first things that tourists ventured upon when visiting Salida.

In 1904, the Denver & Rio Grande railroad implemented the dining car system rendering the Monte Cristo restaurant obsolete. The Monte Cristo was sold to the company that ran the dining cars and Charles was transferred to Pueblo to work at the Union Depot.

Five years later, Charles returned to Salida and took on a ten-year lease of The Denton (formerly the St. Clair), the swankiest hotel in town. Built in 1890 on the corner of 1st and E Streets, it was four stories high, with 88 rooms. It had parlors, billiard rooms, a dining room, and a steam-powered elevator. The hotel even had a sewage drainpipe installed, 870 feet long, that connected to the Arkansas River.

Charles hired on one of the best chefs in Colorado, Ed Goodnight, and a wait staff that previously worked at the Broadmoor in Colorado Springs: "Mr. Catlin cannot fail to make a success of this enterprise, with proper support of Salida people."

After Charles retired from the hotel business, he was appointed Justice of the Peace in 1917 by Chaffee County commissioners. By 1921, Judge Catlin had married 100 couples in Chaffee County:

"He has become so accustomed to the ceremony that he has it thoroughly memorized and he never suffers the least embarrassment even when he feels deep down in his heart one of the 'high contracting parties' is getting the worst of the bargain."

Charles died here in Salida in 1928. In 1941, the Monte Cristo Hotel, along with the Denver & Rio Grande railroad depot, was torn down. The Hotel Denton had been torn down the previous decade.

Twenty-Five

The Footbridge

A hanging footbridge built across the Arkansas River was the scene of one of Salida's worst disasters. It was constructed in 1881 and was located approximately 2 blocks downriver from F Street. The bridge had been built by Miles Mix, local entrepreneur, sometime sheriff, and proprietor of the Mix House. According to the Sanborn Maps, a collection which contains some of the oldest known detailed maps of Salida, the Mix House was on the corner of 1st and E streets and was a boarding house for the Denver & Rio Grande railway workers. Mix built the bridge to make it easier for his tenants to get to and from work. But by 1882, the Mix House had changed hands, and by 1887, it had been demolished. The bridge remained.

Through the years, the bridge was reconstructed and repaired; there was a special committee formed in 1888 that mended the bridge with a cost of $42 to the city. In 1899, a dam broke in Granite sending a torrent of water downriver. By the time it reached Salida, the river was cresting and carrying debris along with it:

"Considerable excitement was caused yesterday by a report that four feet of water was rushing down the river. Big crowds congregated at the F Street Bridge and the D Street suspension bridge. Shortly after 5 o'clock the water rose 6 inches and for several hours a great deal of drift came down. The water was within a few inches of the suspension bridge and many big logs struck it, but inflicted no damage."

The Hanging Bridge

In 1904, the Grand Army of the Republic, an organization of retired Union veterans, planned a Memorial Day parade and celebration for Salida. The parade route would weave through the downtown area, and participants which included the Salida Fire Department, local school kids, and various city officials, would join in, eventually ending up at the Opera House at 129 W. 1st Street where a memorial speech and other tributes would take place. Then:

"Immediately at the close of the services at the Opera House the Post and auxiliary societies will escort the children to the F Street Bridge, where the ceremony will be observed of launching a flower laden ship and scattering flowers on the flowing waters of the Arkansas River, in memory of the Union soldier sailors who were buried at sea during the Civil War."

Over a thousand people were milling about for the Memorial Day celebration. Hazel Lines and her family were on the hanging bridge, along with 20-30 others, watching the festivities upstream. Hazel's older brother Ray (12 at the time) was most likely hanging out with his friends downtown. The ceremony began and everyone on the bridge leaned on the upstream side of it to get a good view when a cable snapped, and the bridge collapsed into the river, taking everyone with it. Keep in mind this happened at the end of May, so the river would have been fast and high from snowmelt.

Most made it out of the water with help from the crowd that was gathered; but four people died that day, including 5-year-old Hazel. Hazel's dad clung to his wife and 2-year-old son Lance; he was able to grasp a rope from the people on the bank, but Hazel was swept downstream. Her body was recovered a short time later.

Charles Lines said of his little girl after, when the scene was still chaotic and people were missing:

"It might have been worse…I am glad her body was recovered, and my heart goes out in sympathy to those whose loved ones sleep in a watery grave."

The body of 8-year-old Esther Morgan was never recovered. 9-year-old Pearl Holland and Mrs. Sarah Thompson were found later on.

After the grief, the blame. The bridge had been known to be unsafe for some time and the families wanted retribution.

R.A. Holland, Charles Lines, and Dave Morgan, fathers of the three children who drowned, sued the city a year later and the case was tried. The verdict? The city was found to be blameless since the bridge was being used as a grandstand rather than a conveyance to get to and fro across the river.

The Memorial Day footbridge disaster instigated the replacement of the wooden F Street Bridge, giving us the stone bridge we have today. A new cable bridge was built further down at C Street to replace the D Street foot bridge. The new bridge, still under construction, claimed a life when 11-year-old Arthur Wilson fell off, struck his head, and drowned in the river.

Twenty-Six

Salida's Music Teacher

Twenty-year-old musician James Ramey was a self-taught virtuoso, being proficient in piano, mandolin, guitar, violin, and voice. After refining his skills at the Chicago Conservatory, he moved with his family to Salida and began seeking work as a music teacher. He placed an ad in the local paper requesting people join in a Saturday afternoon vocal class at the Christian Church where his dad was pastor. It was an evident success; the group's early attendance boasted 50 members: "Professor Ramey has quite an interesting singing class here; the next meeting will be Tuesday night."

For the next decade, James built up his reputation as a music teacher. In 1895, he married Kitty and, after a brief hiatus in Canon City, the Rameys moved into a house on Park Avenue and settled into life in Salida. The 1890s were a particularly productive time for him; he began composing music in earnest and one of his first compositions was entitled, appropriately, 'Salida.'

Besides teaching and composing, James was a performer. In 1899, in an effort to raise funds for the Christian Endeavor Society, the Christian Church held a musical entertainment which they called

'The Phantasma.' The theatrical title was probably in reference to the stereopticon (or slide projector) show that was part of the evening's program. Most significantly, James Ramey's juvenile orchestra, made up of kids playing violins, guitars, mandolins, and piano, made its debut into Salida society. It was an all-Ramey revue, with the kids performing songs like 'Stay with 'em, Oom Paul, You're All Right,' 'Prospector's Reward,' and 'Grand Canon March.'

James and his brother also started a band, the Ramey Mandolin Club, and they were kept busy at entertainments around the area. One evening saw them performing a concert at Mrs. Jackson's Hotel in Poncha Springs and offering up the "best music the Ramey boys could furnish." And James, along with his band, participated in one memorable 4th of July in Howard: besides a picnic, running and relay races, and bucking bronco contests, the Ramey Orchestra performed all night for the denizens of Howard, who stayed up dancing 'til the wee hours.

In 1905, the Methodist Church held a stereopticon show with the catchy title 'Ten Nights in a Barroom.' It was a morality tale of sorts, "a splendid object lesson on the awful results of falling into the temptation of money-making by the saloon." James Ramey's orchestra provided the background music for the entertainment.

'Ten Nights' would have been a popular show in Salida at the time. The previous year selling alcohol to women was outlawed in the city of Salida. The local temperance union was a force to be reckoned with here. Besides having a chapter in town, they regularly drove their doctrine at the local churches.

At this time, the Salida City Council also enacted an ordinance banning music in the local taverns. According to the ordinance, music was to be banned "where lewd persons assemble for dancing."

James may have been conflicted about the music ban. He understood the transcendent beauty of a good piece of music, no matter where it came from. James wrote the following anecdote about Carrie Nation which underscores that point. Recall that Nation was a fiery member of the national temperance movement, known for smashing up bars with her hatchet:

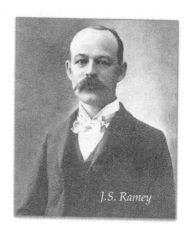

J.S. Ramey

"It is said that a close friend of the late Carrie Nation, once found her standing with bowed head and reverential posture near a low drinking place, intently listening to the soft strains of melody and harmony as they drifted out from the building. Upon being mildly reproached by her friend, Mrs. Nation calmly replied, 'The music comes out pure.'"

The music ban did not last, perhaps because James ran for city council in 1909 and won, eventually serving on council for 25 years. At any rate, prohibition was soon after enacted, which sent all the 'lewdness' underground.

During this time, James was a prolific composer of music. In 1917, one of his pieces was in the running to replace Colorado's state song. At the time, the state song was Francis Atlee's 'Where the Columbines Grow' which was controversial in that it never mentions the word Colorado. Ramey's song 'The Skies Are Blue in Colorado' became a strong contender to replace it and Representative A.E. Wright introduced a bill declaring it to be considered the official state song. It was not to be; at the end of February 1917, both the Colorado senate and house voted to retain the 'Columbines' song.

In 1928, James wrote a series of articles for the Salida Mail entitled 'Short Music Talks.' These essays were a master course on Ramey's strength – music theory – and he wrote nimbly, albeit esoterically. This is just a small sample from one of the articles:

"The Parallel major and minor scales have the same key-tone, but different signatures; for instance A is the relative minor of C major, and the parallel minor of A major, etc. A little concentrated thought and a few examples worked out will fix and establish this important point of theory firmly in the mind. To quickly determine the signature of the parallel minor, deduct three sharps, or add three flats to the signature of the major. With the one and two sharp keys deduct them and make up the number three by adding the difference in flats."

Ramey continues, adding in phrases of similar content, only changing the music key note and the number of additions or subtractions of sharps and flats. With zero irony, he finishes up his article with "I trust that I have made this subject clear, as it is usually confusing to most students."

In another of his articles, James touched on the nature of music and included commentary on the music form Jazz. There is a certain amount of foresight in his response, and given the racial climate of the era, he would have been in the minority in his defense of Jazz:

"Frequently, I am asked the question: What do you think of Jazz? In answer, I must say that I know very little about it. However, we must admit that it seems to please the rank and file and, as one of the main attributes of music is to afford pleasure, it must be credited with a certain amount of merit. I believe that the ultra-modern 'Jazz' in its chaotic and distorted form, is really a protest and demand for something truly 'distinctly American.' I believe in time it will evolve and settle down into a system that will be recognized as legitimate and in keeping with the American spirit."

James died in 1934. In 1938, five years after prohibition was repealed, the Salida City Council once again banned music in Salida's bars:

"The City Council last night adopted on first reading an ordinance to prohibit music of any kind in taverns. This will include musical instruments, played by hand, and mechanically operated radios, Missouri fiddlers, orchestras, pianists and each and every other kind of music and swing. Even the singing of 'Sweet Adeline' is barred."

Twenty-Seven

The Tenderfoot Magazine

In 1909, the Salida High School senior class launched a literary magazine and christened it The Tenderfoot. Published monthly during the school year, it sold for 10 cents and included class photos, highlighted student essays and fictions, and recorded the accomplishments of the school's athletic teams.

The popularity of The Tenderfoot was evident from its inception. In 1910, the Salida Mail reported that "the success of the Tenderfoot is something phenomenal, reaching such popularity with all that an Annual is being planned."

School sports were just coming in to their own, in this early part of the 20th century, and with no organized state system, schools kept their own sporting records. In May of 1910, the girls' basketball team was crowned champion of Western, Central, and Southern Colorado:

"The Salida basketball girls have made one of the most excellent records in the history of the S.H.S. Out of eleven games played, they have won ten and have scored in all, 228 points to their opponents' 76 ... By defeating Aspen and Gunnison from the West, Canon City from the South, and Monte Vista and Alamosa from Central

Colorado, Salida High School feels that she can rightfully claim the championship from those portions of the State and up to the present time, no one has dared to dispute the claim."

GIRLS' BASKETBALL TEAM – Champions of Western, Central and Southern Colorado.   *Photo by HAY*

The girls were not the only ones winning championships. Boys' basketball also had a successful season in 1910, winning 12 out of 14 games. SHS had school spirit, so much so that the Tenderfoot editor put out a request for 'yells':

"Once upon a time, way back in the [18]90s, somebody organized the Salida High School, and with it they wrote some yells and songs which our ancestors must have used during the Age of Chivalry. At any rate, these same old yells have been handed down to us through several generations and now the parts that have not been forgotten are worn out completely. Do, for goodness sake, sit down and write us something that we can make a noise with! There is nothing that does more to make a team feel like playing its best, than a lot of good old enthusiastic, rollicking, blood-thrilling yells and we are going to have them at the next basketball game or die in the attempt."

One of the students at Salida High during this time was Omer Divers. In 1911, Omer was elected vice president of his freshman class and later played football and baseball for SHS. In 1912, he, along with fellow student Arthur French, built a wireless radio system:

"Mr. Divers and Arthur French are busy perfecting [their] station and making all the apparatus …

Nina Churcher and Omer
Divers at the Crater

There will be no doubt as to its working facilities, as there is one such station now in Denver which was constructed by Mr. Divers last year, and makes perfect communication with Colorado Springs and other points about the state."

Omer went on to great things: After graduation, he enrolled at Carnegie Tech and played quarterback for their football team. He enlisted in the U.S. Army and became one of the first flying radio sergeants in the Army Signal Corps. After the war, he was instrumental in setting the world's motorcycle speed record with Glenn Curtis and he became chief mechanic for Eddie Rickenbacker during that legend's Indianapolis 500 heyday. Omer later became a barnstormer and traveled across the country performing in flying shows.

The Tenderfoot staff also published editorials in their literary magazine. Many of these included inspirational advice, vital for the underclassmen:

"Remember that the greater part of your high school career is not to train you that you may make a living, it is to teach you to enjoy life; to see and know the best in things, whether it be in business or in the school or at home. Remember it isn't the knowledge that you have acquired from books that is fitting you to take your place in the world and hold your own -- it is the training in learning that you have acquired which makes you capable of learning what you are to be taught, and retaining it. It makes you capable of keeping up with the times, for in this age of innumerable new things, the one who is behind the times is pushed out of the race and the world moves along without him ... Last of all, treat the new, small, wee Freshies kindly. Remember how you were treated and treat them likewise so that the number shall survive and the school prosper."

In these early years, it was a tough business staying in school until graduation, particularly if you were a boy. Back then there was no stigma attached to dropping out. Sometimes it was a necessity for a teenager to drop out and help the family make ends meet. Sometimes it was more attractive to drop out and get a job to start making some money of one's own.

The SHS graduating class of 1915 had a total of 26 kids, and only three of those were boys. These three (Hank, Bill, and Dusty) formed a 'Triple Alliance' and wrote an essay for that year's annual which examined their senior year of survival:

"Why did we survive? That is a question to which not one of us can give a definite answer. In the secret recesses of our souls, we have attempted to find the reason, but as yet we have arrived at no conclusion as to how and why we really did reach our present point

HENRY SANDUSKY: "*Hank.*"

Alas! he lacks a middle name
On which to hinge his baseball fame!

FRANKLIN WILLARD WOODY:

"*Bill.*"

He is one of those whom we may not offend. He is one of the three. Sweet face, don't you think?

GEORGE HOWARD RHODES:

"*Dusty.*"

Isn't that "Georgie" part rich? Got his hair nice and slick, hasn't he? It doesn't look quite so nice when he's winning a game for the team, and the score result is dubious.

of desperation. Of course, as freshmen, this problem did not particularly annoy us, for we had about the usual number of companions in misery. [By sophomore year] we formed a Triple Alliance for self-defense ... and even though the girls tormented us a great deal by such inhuman tortures as mussing our sleek pompadours and making us see at least a dozen of them home, we nevertheless managed to retain our sweet dispositions. We then received our well-earned diplomas and were glad to say that we had survived to graduate with the suffragette class of 1915."

The death knell for The Tenderfoot (though it later made a comeback as the Tenderfoot Times, the student newspaper) occurred with the 1913 inaugural issue of Le Resume, named by student Arthur French.

School superintendent Edgar Kesner addressed the transformation of The Tenderfoot into the yearbook Le Resume. This, from the 1913 Le Resume's dedication:

"An Arabian legend tells of a bird that, after it had lived a certain time would set fire to itself and be consumed, then arise from its ashes more beautiful than ever. So from the ashes of *The Tenderfoot* has arisen the Annual. May it prove a worthy successor is the wish of your superintendent and friend."

Twenty-Eight

It Is Worthwhile

In 1894, a group of Salida's brightest townswomen formed the Tuesday Evening Club, an organization dedicated to the betterment of Salida. Their goal was to create a library, and the first order of business was to educate themselves.

This, from a speech given by Lillian Mosgrove, a founding member of the Tuesday Evening Club:

"From the start we were ambitious. Adopting the motto 'Operae pretium est' we tried to do worthwhile things. Our first study was a university extension course in general history. Then followed in turn the study of literature and music of the different countries. We wrote papers, gave book reviews, discussed the trend of modern literature and studied parliamentary law. Everyone was interested and everyone worked."

These ladies embraced education and advocated for a library for the people of this town. It was all for the greater good. They taught themselves library science those first years in preparation for the duties that come with running a library.

Soon, the club began to acquire books for their library. Mary Ridgway, the first Club president, writes:

"I went to Denver and made the rounds of the few second-hand bookstores, and, oh joy, found some histories within my price and enough for the club. As I remember, they were rather sad and withered looking in their black cloth binding and poor print. But: how proud I felt of them, for they were our books. They belonged to the Tuesday Evening Club."

By 1902, the ladies had acquired around 1,200 books. The Tuesday Evening Club then took the necessary steps for incorporation and the Salida Library Association was formed that same year. The library collection was first housed at the Central School on the corner of D & 3rd and quickly outgrew its space. The collection was then moved to a room near the Disman-Alger block on W. 2nd, then to 306 F, and lastly to the city council rooms at 124 E St. All this time the Tuesday Evening Club members took turns serving as desk clerk to the library

Ruth Spray

cardholders who were checking out books.

With the collection growing year by year, the need was becoming ever greater to build a library to house it. The club began the fundraising necessary for the construction of a library building. They sponsored lectures and chautauquas, and entertained with concerts and musical & comic operas. They even held a Passion Play.

In July of 1905, Ruth Spray, president of the Salida Library Association, wrote a letter to

Andrew Carnegie, the noted library philanthropist, requesting additional funding. Salida's mayor and aldermen, the president of the Board of Trade, and the deputy district attorney all endorsed the creation of a new library, and letters of support were sent to Carnegie. Even the Salida Mail editors reported "Salida wants some of Mr. Carnegie's coin." By that December, a single sentence response was received from Mr. Carnegie's secretary:

SALIDA LIBRARY.

"If the city agrees by resolution of council to maintain a free public library at a cost of not less than $900 a year and provide a site for the building, Mr. Carnegie will be glad to give $9,000 to erect a free public library building for Salida."

The fundraising began in earnest and they eventually raised $6,000 with the help of the community. All that was needed was a suitable site to build the new library.

Mary Ridgway and her husband purchased the site on the corner of 4th and E Streets for $1,200. The cornerstone of Salida granite was laid there in May of 1908 and most of the town turned out for the installation: "The speeches were all bright and interesting and were confined to three minutes each."

Cornerstone laying ceremony at 4th and E Streets.

A box was placed within the cornerstone that contains, among other things, copies of the correspondence between Carnegie and the club, a photo of Salida, and a postcard with an image of the future library. The entire crowd sang 'America' at the closing of the ceremony.

February 1909 marked the opening of the Salida Public Library, built at a cost of $15,000. It was due in large part to the efforts of the Tuesday Evening Club. The Club immediately handed over the library to the city and council accepted. A dedication was held in May of that year, celebrating the newest jewel of Salida.

What these ladies accomplished was a remarkable achievement when one thinks about the time and the place in society that women occupied back then. Consider this: a woman could get a library built but she couldn't get a drink in this town. It was against the law, being a violation of city ordinance:

"It shall be unlawful for any woman to loiter about or frequent any saloon, or to drink spirituous, vinous, or malt liquors in a saloon, or at a public bar...Any one violating the provisions of this section shall, upon conviction thereof, be fined in any sum not less than three dollars nor more than one hundred dollars."

Not that the ladies would have taken a drink. The notorious Carrie Nation was a guest at one of the chautauquas that the Tuesday Evening Club sponsored in 1908. Nation was a temperance advocate who used to destroy bars with a hatchet she carried with her. She was introduced by Ruth Spray, Library Association president, who endorsed her technique of 'saloon smashing,' as it were. The local newspaper was on the fence about it, when they critiqued her visit:

"Whether we approve of her works or not, Mrs. Nation is one of the greatest agitators of the day and is stirring up the people. She is undoubtedly an agitator of the John Brown stamp ... She sold her books [at the end of her speech] and gave a hatchet with each purchase."

It should also be noted that one of the books in the library's early collection was the volume *The Liquor Problem in All Ages* which included the memorable quote:

"We are still in the midst of a great battle. The forces of alcohol were never before so compactly and powerfully organized in Great Britain or the United States as now. Their leagues are everywhere ... No great permanent improvement in the condition of the country can be expected until government declares that the liquor traffic is an evil which must be put down in the interest of society."

When you're at Friday Afternoon Club this week, raise a glass to the Tuesday Evening Club. They gave Salida this special library.

Twenty-Nine

Salida Red Cross

Worrld War I pulled in with a tide of death and destruction; when it pulled back, a deadlier tide of influenza had begun to wash over the entire world.

The convergence of WWI with one of the deadliest pandemics on record had one bright note: the American Red Cross was at its strongest, reinforced by a large cadre of volunteer nurses. Here in Salida the Tuesday Evening Club, who were the founders of the library, started a Red Cross chapter in an effort to support the troops who were headed overseas.

The first organizational meeting was held April 1917 in the assembly hall at the library. Church leaders, medical professionals, and local club and lodge members all attended, voting in Ben Disman, owner of a popular clothing store here in town, as head.

The Red Cross Hospital and Denver & Rio Grande Hospital immediately began training women and girls in the techniques of first aid and nursing.

Later that month, the first recruits from Salida were headed to World War I. They were seen off by everyone in town, including Civil

War and Spanish-American War veterans. It was a moment to witness in Salida's history:

"All Salida turned out Sunday afternoon to say goodbye to the twelve boys who left for Pueblo to enlist in the United States navy, the first body of volunteers to leave the city. F Street was crowded from the depot to nearly First Street and around the boys at the depot was a great crowd of friends and well-wishers."

At this time, the United States government appointed a council to direct the Red Cross and they put out a directive to all chapters across the country. Wounded soldiers required tools for their recovery: bandages, gauze, surgical dressings, sheets, pillowcases, convalescent gowns, just about anything that a hospital needed to aid in healing. The Salida Red Cross sew-a-thon began:

"Nimble fingers are busy and sewing machines are humming in the Red Cross headquarters, where a corps of women work from 9 o'clock in the morning till 5 o'clock in the evening every week day, preparing material for the hospital and emergency stations at the front."

By the end of October, the ladies had sewn or knitted over 11,000 bandages or garments for the war wounded. They were just getting started: 200 pounds of knitting yarn soon arrived in Salida for the local Red Cross chapter and a free knitting class was held at the Red Cross rooms in the Disman-Alger block at 134 F Street: "The yarn will be supplied free. Knitting needles can be had of Miss Bertie Roney on F Street."

Patriotism was sweeping across Salida and the country. James Ramey, Salida's popular music teacher, published a new song to get everyone in the spirit, aptly titled "Our Uncle Sam." It was sung by his daughter Lenore at the first patriotic meeting held in Salida after the U.S. joined the war.

The tide was about to turn. One year later, another of Ramey's daughters, Laura, would be dead from influenza.

There are several theories as to how the 1918 Pandemic started. What is most certain is that the spread began at an army base in Kansas in the spring of 1918. Influenza infected American soldiers who, on their way to World War I, passed it on to Europe. This was

On Sunday, May 19, 1918, a huge Red Cross parade was held in Salida. The parade featured the Salida Band, a group of Civil War veterans, the local boy scouts, the families of enlisted soldiers, and lastly, the Salida Red Cross chapter, which included the Junior Red Cross. This last group consisted of 180 white-clad women who marched "in perfect formation." This image was probably taken before the parade that day and everyone is posed in front of the newly built Salida Library. Dr. George Curfman, D&RG hospital chief surgeon, is at front center, the first gentleman on the left.

the first wave of the pandemic. Once it circulated through Europe, it came back to America on its second wave later that autumn.

Flu hit Salida like a freight train. Out of nowhere, on October 15th, there were more than 200 people sickened with influenza and two people had died. Three days later, five more had died. The local hospitals were overrun and the Hotel Denton (on the corner of 1st and E) was turned into a makeshift ward. The next day, 73 patients filled the hotel, along with a convoy of nurses and emergency staff. Even this was not enough to care for all of the ill:

"Whole families are down with the disease and have no one to nurse them. All the nurses in Salida have worked until they are worn out and still the call comes for help ... The women of Chaffee County are appealed to in the name of DUTY to volunteer their services. Danger must be ignored."

The comparison can be made here of the heroics of soldiers on the battlefield and the heroics of nurses during an epidemic. The bravery of each can be tallied, but it is a certain fact that a nurse going into battle against an unknown disease, without a weapon, has a certain rarified courage not seen in any average person.

A week after the flu hit Salida, eighteen people were dead and 330 people were ill. Doctors and nurses were working around the clock. The Red Cross was handing out pneumonia jackets, archaic garments made from oiled silk that were used for warming the ill. The more expensive jackets had tubing within that circulated warm water around the torso. The chairman of the Red Cross committee, Mrs. Garrelts, spent her days searching the county for nurses to help during the crisis.

Salida went into quarantine. Schools and churches effectively shut down. It was a desperate time:

"Influenza is fastening a deeper grip on Salida every hour and the doctors cannot see an approach to the end."

Dr. George Hardin Curfman, chief surgeon at the Denver & Rio Grande Hospital, was on the front lines when the 1918 Flu Pandemic swept through Salida.

Keep in mind that the epidemic occurred before centralized heating and electric blankets. Home heat was dependent upon keeping the fires in the hearth or stove going. Father Gallagher spent one morning chopping wood for a family who were all bedridden. There had been no heat in the house before he arrived.

We were not alone in the crisis. Denver had reportedly run out of coffins by this time, in an effort to dispose of the dead. Gunnison was one of the few towns in Colorado that avoided the full wrath of the pandemic. They had set up road blocks into their town and anyone in violation was either imprisoned or fined.

Despite the panic, there were moments of selflessness. The Salida Red Cross had formed an influenza committee to manage the logistics of the epidemic, particularly at the hospitals. Members were charged with finding replacement nurses, laundering linen, filling pantries and larders, and collecting funds to keep all of the services running. Local madam Laura Evans deployed some of her workers to help with nursing the ill. Any extra food was gathered for families unable to leave their houses: bread, chicken, eggs, fruit, and jelly were all donated by townsfolk.

Volunteer nurses were everywhere. The hospital alone counted 22 during the crisis. The Salida Mail reported on their condition: "These nurses are wearing out and soon must be relieved. All who can serve are earnestly requested to report to Mrs. Garrelts or at the hospital."

By the first of November, news spread that dogs and cats were carriers of the flu virus. It was immediately mandated that any stray dog or cat would be destroyed, shot by local law enforcement.

And for the next two months, there is no record of the Salida Record and Salida Mail newspapers being published.

The 1918 pandemic struck in a 'W' shaped curve, killing people of all ages. Normal flu strains strike in a 'U' shaped curve, generally killing the young and the elderly, those with more susceptible immune systems. Though they didn't know it at the time, the best defense (before vaccines and herd immunity) was survival through the earlier 1889 flu pandemic. This gave most middle-aged people an immunity against the 1918 pandemic.

About two billion people were living on the planet in 1918. 500 million were infected. 50-100 million people died. Eighty died in Salida.

The quarantine was partially lifted by January 1919, though elementary-age kids were still not permitted back in school. The high school resumed classes but the kids had missed so much work that school started early and ended late, in an effort to catch up.

In March, the quarantine was completely lifted from schools and businesses. It had been 4½ months since the quarantine was declared. Local churches were able to hold services. Younger kids were allowed back in school, but a nurse was present at the school's front door to check for illness. Salidans were still wary; school attendance was light that first day back in session.

Of the eighty Salidans who died that season, local musician James Ramey's daughter Laura was a particularly difficult loss. She was recently married and had come back to town to visit family and friends. She had spent time nursing a family ill with influenza and soon after became ill herself and succumbed:

"[Laura] loved the Red Cross work and at all times was active in helping them but when the dread scourge of Spanish influenza made its appearance on our shores and, sweeping across the country demanded as its toll millions of our people, it was then she found her place in the ranks of men and women who were offering their lives daily in nursing and caring for the victims of the plague. Along with many others her name will be remembered not only on earth, but in Heaven, as one who gave her life that others might live."

Thirty

The Beginning of a Tradition

Thirteen years after the 1904 Memorial Day bridge disaster, Hazel Lines' older brother Ray was drafted into the Army to serve in World War I. An explosive shell killed him on September 18, 1918. His burial took place here in Salida in 1922.

What took so long?

The precedent for bringing home American military dead was not established until the Spanish-American War, and even then not completely. Consider that over 2,500 U.S. soldiers died in the Spanish-American War, but over 100,000 died in the one year our country fought in World War I. There was no protocol for returning all of the bodies of these American soldiers back to home soil. The logistics and cost posed a huge problem for the United States. Air transport dedicated to transporting the dead was non-existent.

On the Western Front in France, these American dead, possibly 70,000, were buried in temporary graves. Accordingly, France set in place a ban that prohibited the removal of bodies from French soil.

What finally changed policy was the voice of the American people. After years of demanding the remains of their soldier sons, the U.S. War Department relented, and once the French ban lifted it took about two years for the remains of 46,000 soldiers to be returned to the U.S. The remainder were left buried in France, at the behest of their families.

Salida held a military funeral on April 23, 1922 in honor of Ray Lines, and to honor the sacrifices of all the men and women who

Ray Lines escort leaving the Presbyterian Church, on the corner of F and Third Streets.

served. It was a grand affair, complete with band, color guard, pastors and pallbearers, military veterans and enlisted men, army nurses, an honor guard, and of course, mourners. There were American flags posted everywhere. Townsfolk gathered at Riverside Park, then marched up to the undertaker's on 1st Street to collect the casket. A service was held at the Presbyterian Church (which was then on the corner of 3rd & F) and afterwards, the casket with escort, along with the huge crowd, proceeded to Fairview Cemetery. Ray was given full military honors, complete with the playing of Taps and a gun salute at his graveside.

Ray Lines being laid to rest at Fairview Cemetery

This would have been an interesting time in America. Soldiers were being given the most patriotic funerals, never before seen in this country. It marked the beginning of our current tradition: to bring home the military dead, no matter the cost.

American Legion Post #64 is named in honor of Ray Lines.

Thirty-One

Salida's First Flight

It is likely that the first plane to take off at an elevation of over 7,000 feet was in Salida, Colorado.

The 4th of July celebration in 1919 was going to be jam-packed with events: baseball games, horse racing, bronc riding, fireworks, boxing tournaments, and something special: the first aeroplane flight in Salida. At the time, most people in Chaffee County had never seen an airplane in flight before. The program would showcase two flights a day: one in the afternoon, and then an "illuminated flight with fireworks" each night.

For months, the town was buzzing with excitement. Nearly every eligible female was dreaming of going up into the air with pilot Harry B. Crewdson. The planning committee was promising flights with the young pilot and they were immediately inundated with letters of intent from interested ladies requesting consideration. The local paper headlined: "Girls Insist on Aeroplaning" and the committee chairman commented: "We have no objection to letting a girl go up and do the loop, nose spin, tail dive, and bank fly, because, as the girls explain to us, they should have something to talk about the same as the boys who made flights in war planes."

Upon hearing the news that Crewdson would be the one to entertain Salida with aerial acrobatics, a visitor from out-of-town exclaimed:

"What! Harry B. Crewdson! Why you have the best aviator in the United States. He will do any stunt that any aviator in the world will do. He will try to please the crowd but he will not make a speech. He has less to say than any man I ever knew. But when it comes to flying he can use any style of machine and if necessary he can fly down F Street between the buildings."

Harry Crewdson

In June, the preparations began in earnest at the Salida city fairgrounds, then located just southwest of town. Grandstands were erected and concession booths built; thirty concessionaires were to be stationed at the grounds and thirty more would be in downtown Salida, amidst all the other amusements. In expectation of the large crowds, Poncha Boulevard would be closed off to cars from Salida all the way to Poncha Springs.

The big day arrived, and for fifty cents admission, a crowd of 8,000 people gathered at the fairgrounds to see Harry.

Problems immediately ensued when Harry couldn't get the plane's engine to fire. He and his band of mechanics worked feverishly all day and finally, at 4:30 in the afternoon, Harry B. Crewdson ascended into the sky above Salida. The crowd thrilled as he made three circles to gain altitude and then began his stunts "looping the loop, flying upside down and then straight up, nose-diving, banking, and maneuvering like a bird. He mounted higher and higher into the air until his plane was no larger than an eagle and the sound of his engine could no longer be heard."

In these early days of aviation, pilots were still learning how to fly at elevation, and most would not attempt it. Thinner air density reduces engine horsepower; inevitably, there's less air to mix with the fuel. An aircraft engine will lose about 3.5 percent of its horsepower for every 1,000 feet of elevation gain. At 7,000 feet, 25% of the engine's power is lost automatically. So it follows that the weight of the plane becomes a serious issue for pilots at elevation, particularly at takeoff and landing. Harry's plane that day contained a 250 hp engine, enhancing the weight of the plane. Also, in a high elevation scenario, density altitude factors in. Density altitude is pressure altitude corrected for variations from standard temperatures: as temperature and altitude increase, air density decreases which makes a plane accelerate and climb more slowly.

The heat of that July day, the high altitude of Salida, and the weight of Harry's plane contributed to the disaster that next arose. In view of thousands, pilot Harry Crewdson's plane engine failed when he attempted his descent:

"He volplaned [control dived] within 1,000 feet of the ground, swept over the fair grounds in a large circle and was preparing to ascend again when his engine stopped. He signaled to his mechanics that he was having trouble and would have to descend. He swept again over the track and decided to land outside the grounds but the engine took hold again and he soared over to the aviation field. His engine was working again as he neared the earth and he intended to come within a few feet of the ground, elevate the nose of the plane and ascend to a great height to complete the stunts. At that moment his engine commenced missing. He saw that he must descend and he looked for a favorable place, while he unstrapped himself from the machine to prepare for an accident. The wheels of the plane touched the ground, the right wing tilted to one side and swept the ground, wheeling the plane round until it faced in the opposite direction,

The wreck of Harry Crewdson's plane

AVAITOR CREWDSON July 4ᵗʰ 1919 SALIDA Colo BAD LANDING NO ONE HURT

while the nose of the engine plowed into the earth. The propeller blades snapped like matches and the plane crashed about him like a falling building."

A doctor who was first on the scene peeled a dazed Crewdson from his plane. The force of the crash had thrown his body backwards, sparing his legs from being crushed by the cockpit. His head was then thrown forward and he struck it against the dash of the plane. Miraculously, Harry only suffered a broken nose in the crash.

Harry later spoke about the challenges of high altitude flying:

"In the higher altitudes it is necessary to travel at a higher rate of speed in order to obtain enough resistance to fly. Once in the air, the machine can readily get up the necessary speed, but the danger comes at the moment of alighting. In order to be safe an aviator should be traveling at the rate of 100 miles an hour when the wheels of his plane touch the earth, because if he shuts off his speed when he approaches the earth, the resistance of the air is not sufficient to sustain him and the plane drops like a plummet to the earth. Since he is close to the ground he has no chance to recover as he might when he loses altitude higher up … [T]he fact is none of the aviators will go up nowadays except in the evening, when the sun is low or early in the morning.

"It is too bad I could not give the people all they came to see but my engine was not working properly and it was a bad finish. Aeroplanes are not built to start and alight at this altitude. Once they are up it is comparatively easy but the ascent and descent are trying."

Harry was such a good sport about the crash that Salida wished to repay him for the loss of his plane. The town took subscriptions from the locals and bought Harry a brand new airplane from the Ace Flying Company in New York. It was guaranteed to fly at Salida's elevation.

The aeroplane, christened 'Salida,' was delivered later that August and a great crowd of hundreds of people gathered at the

Denver & Rio Grande depot to witness the arrival and watch as the plane was being assembled.

Harry attempted to fly again but the plane refused to fire. The Ace Flying Company had put their best minds to work on the engine design and installed a "specially constructed high pressure engine" but it was no use. The plane would not fly. Airplane technology was still in its infancy and aviation builders and mechanics were in the process of learning:

"The designers and aviators of the East are unfamiliar with the conditions pertaining to the Western Altitudes. The number of accidents occurring in Denver is out of all proportion to the number in the East and only the most daring aviators will fly in the West."

The airplane 'Salida' was eventually returned to the manufacturer after Harry spent around a week trying to get it to fly. The town of Salida was disappointed, to say the least.

Thirty-Two

Burning Crosses on Tenderfoot

During the 1920s, the Ku Klux Klan made a concerted effort to infiltrate American government in order to advance their agenda of white supremacy. In an effort to appeal to voters, they veiled it in a conservative moralism. Every state was impacted but their biggest presence was in Indiana, Oregon, Kansas, and Colorado. Historian James H. Davis wrote: "After its establishment in Colorado in 1922, the Ku Klux Klan began – under the leadership of Grand Dragon John Galen Locke – to carry out a program of economic and political control in various towns over the state. The organization made certain that channels for dissemination of propaganda and for recruitment were set up. Then it threatened or coerced individuals, groups, and institutions. Finally came attempts to infiltrate into municipal government with the ultimate goal of complete domination."

In January of 1924, the Reverend Ralph Bixel was a vocal supporter of the Klan from his pulpit here in Salida. He was subsequently removed from his position. The Klan gave Bixel a $50 farewell gift, and the letter accompanying it read in part: "We are

A Ku Klux Klan float passes by F and Third Streets during a Salida parade.

proud of your manly and fearless methods of defending righteousness. We want you to know that we sympathize with you for the unwarranted and uncalled for personal abuse you have suffered from vicious and puerile sources, in proclaiming from your pulpit your endorsement of the ideals and principles of our organization."

That January, the KKK burned a cross on Tenderfoot Mountain. It would not be an isolated event and it was happening in other parts of Chaffee County as well. In April of 1924, a cross was burned in Buena Vista at the intersection of Main Street and O'Neal Avenue.

In June, a picnic was held at Mt. Princeton Hot Springs for 2,000 Klansmen and their families. The group was a cross-section of central

Colorado, with groups from not only the Salida area, but the surrounding areas of Gunnison, Alamosa, and Pueblo. The following day, the Klan organized in Buena Vista. 600 were in attendance to witness the installation of 100 members. The group was "all dressed in the white robes and caps [and] made a thrilling scene as the ceremonies progressed."

On June 8th in Salida, at 9:30 in the evening, the KKK paraded down F Street to Sackett, then over to E Street and back up again. The local papers had conflicting numbers as to attendance, with the Salida Record putting the number of marchers at 200; the Chaffee County Republican put it at 600: "...As they started on their silent march through the city's streets, a huge skyrocket shot into the heavens, and an instant later a big cross on Tenderfoot Hill blazed forth, all of which sent a deep thrill through the large crowd lined up on either side of the streets ... The Salida people know that they need have no fear from the KKK as the organization stands for law and order."

Stan Provenza, who grew up here and played for the 1933-35 champion Spartan football team, remembered the Klan's presence here: "There was a Ku Klux Klan, sure enough. They were real strong. I remember as a small boy they would parade up and down the street in their clothes, whatever they wore, with the masks on. They would go up Tenderfoot and they would burn the cross quite often. In fact, I remember sitting on the porch with my neighbor George Smith, and we'd be sitting there and say, 'Well, they're burning the cross now.' It was right about where the 'S' is."

Now that the Klan had begun making its presence felt in Colorado communities, the power grab was on. This, from James

Davis: "The seizure of municipalities was not enough for the Klan; the state government had to be captured also. This was accomplished by obtaining control of the Republican Party, selecting almost all its candidates during the elections of 1924, and making certain the ticket would be successful throughout the state. Once in possession of the executive and legislative branches of Colorado government, the Klan planned to use official acts in furthering its causes on the widest scale possible."

The Klan was successful in gaining multiple seats in local elections across the state and by 1925 a majority of Colorado Senators and Representatives were Klan members. Republican Governor Clarence Morley, an outspoken Klansman and puppet of KKK Grand Dragon John G. Locke, wasted no time in appointing fellow Klansmen into chairmanship positions.

Klan objectives were made clear at the governor's inaugural rally: most pointedly, the Klan wished to pass legislation banning certain immigrants from residing in the state, repeal civil rights laws allowing discrimination against Blacks, ban alcoholic consumption during sacramental activities (an attack on Catholics: no vino = no Mass), and abolish multiple state boards, bureaus, and commissions with the intent of appointing Klansmen to head new boards, bureaus, and commissions.

It did not go as the Klan planned. A total of six Republican senators joined forces with 14 Democratic senators and effectively formed a wall, blocking and killing any bill that the Klan-controlled House put forth. The wall of anti-KKK senators also gave courage to some House members to stand up against Klan members.

One of the Republican senators who made a stand was Salida's own Frank Kelly. Frank and the other senators were blacklisted by

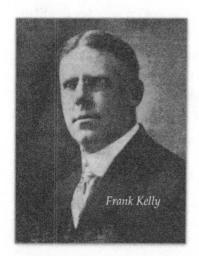

Frank Kelly

the Klan-controlled congress on a daily basis. One of Frank's fellow dissenting senators recalled that each morning a copy of the KKK newspaper would be placed on his desk. The front page had a column called 'Roll of Dishonor' and it listed the names of legislators who had voted against so-called 'patriotic' measures. All readers were urged to never forget their names.

During the 3½ months that the 25th General Assembly was in session, the Republican/Democratic coalition was successful in blocking around 85% of the bills that the Governor and House introduced. The bills to repeal civil rights and outlaw wine at Catholic services never made it out of the House. Governor Morley's entire legislative program had been defeated.

Eventually, Klan influence on Colorado politics was diminished due to the hypocrisy, grifting, and criminal behavior by its members, not only here in Colorado but across the country.

Historian James H. Davis: "The people of Colorado had at last seen the real nature of the Ku Klux Klan as it appeared in their state – an organization dedicated to furthering the selfish ambitions of leaders by debasing every religious or fraternal body as well as every public office useful to that purpose."

Thirty-Three

The Making of Spiral Drive

I n the fall of 1921, R.L. Hampson and his fellow Commercial Club members secretly started clearing a road up Tenderfoot Hill. For the next few months, several men would go up to Tenderfoot Mountain and dig away at the side of the hill building road. They were so stealthy that barely anyone in town knew it was happening.

By February of 1922, Tom Nevens had spilled the beans at a Lion's Club meeting as to what Hampson and his friends were up to. The Commercial Club was a "close corporation and no invitations were issued" to help dig road but the Lions paid no heed to that and decided at once to help out. Everyone wanted to have a stake in the project, but would they actually help with the digging? Tom Nevens immediately rebutted with a 'money where your mouth is' comment: "Come out with a pick and shovel and let pep and service have a holiday. We have all the bosses we need. We want nothing but hand-picked pickmen."

The mayor of Salida issued a proclamation a week later:

"Washington's Birthday ... a legal holiday, offers an opportunity to the citizens of Salida to do some real, constructive work in the upbuilding of the community. Therefore, it is requested that all businesses, which can conveniently do so, be closed and those citizens who desire to do so are urged to assist in the building of Tenderfoot Road."

About 150 people turned out for the holiday and cleared a good quarter mile of road.

Not to be outdone, on March 24th it was 'Railroad Day on the Hill.' Railroad men (representing all the railroad brotherhoods) "cut long stretches of sidehill, filled up several gullies, and built a bridge, bringing the road around the first hill in sight of Salida .... [then] the ladies' auxiliaries of the railroad organizations were on hand with hot dog sandwiches and coffee and kept the workers in good cheer. Joining the railroad men were several farmers and for the first time in the history of Salida, business men, railroad men, and farmers have united in putting a project over."

Steam shovel making progress on Spiral Drive

During this time, R.L. Hampson wrote the song

'The Tenderfoot Road' and sang it at a Lion's Club meeting. The song was "full of pep and made a splendid campaign song." Incidentally, Hampson was the chairman of the Tenderfoot Road Committee, in charge of all activities on Tenderfoot.

A gentle rivalry formed when Railroader's Wednesdays and Businessmen's Thursdays were designated to see who could accomplish more with the road building.

And to raise funds for the effort, the ladies' auxiliaries of the railroad organizations set up dances, entertainments, and 'home cooking sales' which, over the months, raised hundreds of dollars.

Then Warden M.P. Capp from the Buena Vista reformatory boasted: "Give me one day and I will finish the road for you." The Denver & Rio Grande Railroad donated the use of a train to transport around 150 inmates to and from Salida to work on the road. At the end of March, the inmate crew, along with the help of Salida's townsfolk, had completed not all, but over half the road.

April 20th was designated Elks Day on Tenderfoot. The call was broadcast: "Every stray elk who drifts into Salida will be harnessed and put to work." It turned out to be one of the most productive days yet:

"Nearly 200 men were on Mount Tenderfoot with the Salida Elks yesterday and the biggest amount of work done in any one day except [by] the reformatory boys was the result. The road has now swung round in the front so that those working on it can be seen from Salida... Picks and shovels were flying aplenty. Chalk Dinkins was on hand at noon with one of his famous luncheons ... And after the day's work, the Elks and their workers were invited to attend a dance at the Rink. It was well attended and a good time was enjoyed [by all] with regular intermissions for picking water blisters that developed during the day on the hands of the workers."

Work was progressing steadily. Then on July 1st, 150 Denver & Rio Grande employees walked off their jobs at the railroad. It was the start of the Great Railroad Strike of 1922.

This nationwide strike was instigated by railroad labor organizations to protest wage reductions for railway workers across the country. But happily for Salida, these men were now free to work on Tenderfoot Road.

By mid-July, thanks to the efforts of the railroad strikers, the road was nearly complete. And by September, the Salida Chamber of Commerce was taking out-of-towners up to the top of Tenderfoot to show off the panoramic views of Salida.

In October of 1922, Professor Elmore Petersen of Colorado State University visited Salida and had this to say about our town:

"Salida presents an unusual manifestation of the results of actual cooperative effort. One of these days, her 'Tenderfoot Spiral Drive' will be nationally famous. It is an automobile boulevard which winds around the cone-shaped Tenderfoot Mountain just opposite the city, forming a cork-screw to the top, 600 feet above the streets below. From this summit the view of Salida itself, the Arkansas River Valley, the Sangre de Christo and Collegiate ranges of mountains, is too much for words. And over it all spread the snowy wings (literally of snow) of The Angel of Shavano such as may be seen nowhere else in all the world ... This road is entirely the product of cooperative effort and not one dollar has been spent for labor, excepting what money was donated to the cause .... The next time anyone in your town crabs around that there is nothing the local chamber of commerce can do, I respectfully refer you to Salida, that has struck a stride worthy of emulation."

Thirty-Four

The 1929 Air Circus

Ten years after the first semi-successful high elevation flight occurred here in Salida, the American Legion decided to build an airport. The impetus was to send mail by airplane. Airports were springing up all over the West and plane companies were being offered contracts to pick up and deliver mail across the Front Range and the Colorado mountains to points beyond.

Spurred on by the romance of flying and the daring of the early pilots, pioneer air mail service officially began in Colorado in May 1926 with a route between Denver and Cheyenne. Aviation historian Nolie Mumey wrote: "This new direct airmail service permitted Coloradans to send mail to either coast in a single day."

Salida wanted to be a part of it, and the Ray Lines Post of the American Legion set to work. In early June of 1929, the Legion bought a 4,000-foot long airfield for $2,250. These 130 acres were located next to the present day Chaffee County Fairgrounds: "The field purchased by the Legion is naturally level and free from rocks and obstructions. Very little work will be needed to make a first class landing field of this site."

Planes gather for the Air Show

On June 25th, history was made when an Eaglerock (a popular barnstorming plane) piloted by Red Mosier of Pikes Peak Air Commerce successfully lifted off and "landed three points" at the new Salida Legion Airport.

In celebration of the new airfield, an Air Circus was planned for the 4th of July. Pilots from all over were invited to the celebration. A Ford Tri-Motor, a large transport plane which featured three Wright radial engines, was expected for the big event. Also, a Ryan Brougham plane, the sister ship to Lindbergh's Spirit of St. Louis, was flying in. Each plane would offer rides to Circus-goers.

The highlight of the circus was to be an airmail plane landing and picking up Salida's first ever shipment of mail by air. The Chamber of Commerce and the Salida Legion were giving away free envelopes to Salidans who wanted to have a piece of mail on the historic first airmail flight out of Salida. The only cost was the airmail stamp: just 5 cents.

Besides the Air Circus, other events planned during the celebration included Denver & Rio Grande Shopcraft Band concerts at Alpine Park, daylight fireworks, golf tournaments, and the

Y&R Airways Eaglerock plane

Hillman Stock Company of Monte Vista performing plays "under the auspices of the Legion."

The Y&R Auto Company, located at 300 F Street, had recently diversified out by purchasing an Eaglerock biplane and opened Salida's first airline, Y&R Airways. The inaugural flights of the fledgling airline would be held at the Air Circus and they would give rides to passengers in the new Eaglerock to celebrate their inception.

The big day arrived, and on July 4th the Salida Legion Airport was formally dedicated with a bottle of water melted from snow off the figure of the Angel of Shavano. Besides the Ford Tri-Motor plane and the Brougham single engine plane, daredevil Jimmy Donohue thrilled in his Eaglerock stunt plane: "He made three parachute jumps from a plane, did wing walking and crawled over all parts of his plane in the air ... He had planned to leap from Ivy Baldwin's balloon but it failed to go up after having been inflated."

The real star of the show ended up being Salida native and 1916 Salida High School graduate Lieutenant Emmett O'Connor. After getting leave from his base commander in Riverside, California, Emmett flew into Salida in his Douglas O2K and performed for the crowd: "Lt. O'Connor thrilled the crowds with his stunt flying. He put the plane through all the stunts in the book, not forbidden by army rules. The stunts were equaled to the best done anywhere."

It was later recorded that Salida sent approximately sixty pounds of airmail to Colorado Springs, where it was then transferred to a Western Air Express plane and sent to points beyond. The Air Mail Bulletin later lauded Salida: "Officials and citizens of Salida are to be congratulated on their airmindedness and foresight."

After the Air Circus, the buzz of flight was still in the air in Salida. Pilot Clark Carr opened a Y&R Airways flying school which saw huge increases in student participation that summer. Clark began to be known for his daredevil antics in Salida, doing tailspins and loop-de-loops over town: "Pilot Carr, the 'Flying Fool,' is more than delighted when going through these stunts and you'll always find him in high spirits after a good flight … If you really want something to talk about, go out to the airport and for a ride with Mr. Carr."

Y&R Airways was a short-lived enterprise, and by the next year, Clark Carr was living back in Albuquerque, New Mexico, his home state. He went on to great things, establishing the Carco Air Service, known as the 'Atomic Airline,' and became one of the most important figures in New Mexico aviation. Clark has a road named after him in Albuquerque: the Clark Carr Loop.

Thirty-Five

The Hermit of Arbor Villa

In 1879, young Frank Gimlett moved with his family from Illinois and settled in Garfield, Colorado. In his youth, Frank worked with his dad around the Monarch Mining District. Through the years, father and son became successful miners; among other interests, they had part ownership in the famous Columbus Mine, a successful mine which, over its life span, produced millions in ore profits.

Frank married Gertrude in 1897 and with some money and a dream, they moved down to Salida. By 1903, Frank was setting up his business enterprise, the Salida Wood & Lumber Supply Company, situated between 2nd & 3rd next to the Denver & Rio Grande narrow gauge railroad tracks. His business was successful, responsible for building over ten homes in Salida, including the Terraces on the corner of 4th and D streets. He also built 129 & 139 W. 3rd, originally slated to become a theatre, but Frank sold the buildings to the Salida Auto Company.

Frank fulfilled his wish to run a box office and purchased the Salida Opera House at 129 W. 1st, changing its name to the Empress

Theatre. Vaudeville shows were the specialty and he kept the schedule fresh; the pictures changed every Monday, Wednesday, and Friday.

But, as it usually does, life took a turn. By the 1930s, Frank was fighting off debtors and struggling with the aftermath of a fire at his business. Bad luck and bad business practices, and the Great Depression, all played a part in his turn of fortune. And he began to miss the old days back at Garfield.

Frank soon abandoned his wife and business dealings in Salida and set up a homestead at Arbor Villa, located about a mile below Garfield. He then rebranded himself 'The Hermit.'

The Hermit began to live the prospecting life once again. When he wasn't panning for gold in the mountain streams, he set himself up

as a roadside attraction up at the top of Monarch Pass where he sold postcards depicting the good old days.

He wrote about his new life up in the mountains and published an entertaining 9-volume epic *Over Trails of Yesterday*, which were reminiscences of these days gone by. It was curmudgeonly written, these stories about the Monarch mining industry and the immigrants who lived there. The Hermit couldn't turn back time:

"Today I sit alone in the solitude of the Rockies, my habitation on the main street of a once boom town. Not a shingle or board remains to mark the spot where millions of feet once trod past my cabin door. Now and then a tourist journeys by with just a hello, solely bent on curiosity and seeing among the historical ruins some token from the wrecks of the dreams of old pioneers, the relics, but incidents after all to the people of modern days, where sentiment has died."

During this time, the Hermit often made trips to Washington D.C., advocating congress to return the country back to the gold standard. He viewed the future with "great alarm" and proposed that America "deflate gold to its old value and remove the billions of inert useless gold bullion in the vaults of the Nations … for those Pagans of the East who do not care for the motto 'In God We Trust' stamped on their money. [L]et them have the germy, microby, dog-eared and flimsy paper, but see to it that it be backed by 100% gold and silver, so in case we Christians get a hold of it, we can redeem it in honest dollars."

Towards the end of his life, Frank Gimlett served as Salida's Santa Claus. During the 1940s, the Hermit would dress up as Santa and come into town on the Denver & Rio Grande narrow-gauge train. The children would greet him there and they would all walk up to the theatre and spend the day watching cartoons and celebrating.

The Hermit died in 1952 at the age of 77. He was one of Salida's most memorable characters and is best remembered for his poignant and humorous writing:

"Now I have reached the end of the trail, and while I do not see the pot of gold at the rainbow's end, I do see where the clouds are fringed with silver and the sunsets turn to gold atop the great Divide. I see through the dusk of the evening the mines high up on the mountains and the prospectors claims they are impregnated with silver and gold ... Here lies the land of the whiskered prospector, and before I close eulogizing he and his ilk, I want to pay tribute to those old pioneer women who kept romance alive. How love survived and they ever succeeded in planting a kiss on the lips of those gnarled, tobacco-matted, booze-flavored, soup-stained, whiskered and long-spreading 12-inch mustachioed prospectors has always been a mystery to me, and here and now I favor a statue be erected in the halls of fame, honoring these savers of romance under such terrific handicaps."

Thirty-Six

Leonidas and His Spartans

Harold White came to Salida in 1930 and signed on as the head coach of the Salida Spartans. Then the stars aligned.

During the early days of his coaching career, Coach White taught his Spartans the best way to outmaneuver their opponents, who typically outweighed Salida players on average about 20 pounds. The Spartan star quarterback, Frankie Gentile, weighed a nimble 130 pounds throughout his high school career. Football had to become a mental game for the Spartans, not just a rough and tumble assault towards the goal posts.

In 1932, Coach White's work began paying off. The Spartans made it to the State semi-final game, where they were pitted against the Trinidad Miners. But their dreams of a State Championship were dashed that year when they lost 12-0. Most of the Spartan squad were ill with the flu and struggled during this last game. But put this loss aside: the season was a huge accomplishment. The Spartans had scored a season total 234 points to their opponents 32. For the first time in school history, the Spartans became South Central League Champions.

It was their first taste of Colorado football glory and this excitement spread into town, which needed the boost. The Great Depression was gripping Salida, just like everywhere else in America. And Salida took notice of its newest rising star:

"The best known man about town just at present is a tall, blonde-haired, athletic-looking young man who answers to the name of Harold A. White. Young White played some football with his high school team but his work was not particularly noticed until he began playing in the Big Ten wearing the colors of Northwestern University. White has played against the famous Four Horsemen and many other gridiron celebrities of a few seasons ago. Before graduation, Whitey transferred to Utah University where he fell under the tutelage of the famous Ike Armstrong and helped coach Armstrong's freshman squad."

Excitement began to build for the Spartans 1933 season. Salida exploded out of the gate in their first game against Olathe. One spectator described it as a 'nervous breakdown' of a game as Salida trounced Olathe 55-0. The Spartans began to roll, next defeating Monte Vista 8-0 and Colorado Springs 32-0.

At the end of October, Salida was scheduled to play Canon City in the annual fall classic:

"Nothing can stop 'em now. Nothing but a Halloween spook, or the jinx, or a goblin. The Spartans have the championship of the conference in the bag." More than 500 people boarded a special

1933 Spartans

State Football Champions 1933

Denver & Rio Grande booster train that took them to Canon City where they watched the Spartans wallop Canon 21-0.

Salida soon had the best record in the league, shutting out every one of their opponents except Centennial (Salida still beat them 7-6). Individual Spartans began to be noticed by the local press.

In the game against Trinidad, at the end of November, "Scudder, spark plug of the line, in spite of an injury to his head which temporarily sent him to the land of the birdies of floating clouds late in the game, refused to leave the field and continued to make his presence felt during the afternoon ... [and] Oliver Brenton, a freshman, has been phenomenal ... Having the build of a natural ball lugger, Brenton is a powerful line crasher who can't be hurt." The Spartans erased Trinidad with a 7-0 win and were again crowned South Central League Champions.

It was on to the State Championships where Salida would play against the Loveland Indians in an away game and "the entire Junior-Senior student body led by the High School band and the pep club gave the Spartans a rousing send-off at the train and returned to school in time for their fifth period classes." Those who didn't ride to Loveland with the team stayed here in town where the game was broadcast live to an at-capacity house at the Empress Theatre (formerly the Salida Opera House) on 1st Street.

On a beautiful December day, the Spartans conquered:

"Winding up a perfect grid season, the Salida Spartans disposed of their tenth consecutive opponent by running over the Loveland Indians 26-7 to win the State High School Football Championship for the first time in the history of the school. The locals clearly outplayed the heavier Indians on both offense and defense and the fact that four different players made the Spartans four tallies indicates that the locals do not have a one-man team. If one listened to the broadcast of the game at the Empress Theatre he might sometimes think it was a basketball contest. 'Scudder knocks down the ball,' was heard so often it became funny."

Subsequently, Coach White became the most popular guy in town:

"If there are any halos to be hung on the heads of anyone, Coach White should have the biggest and brightest. It was a great day for him ... It was his coaching and his good fellowship with the boys that clinched the victories one by one."

Needless to say, the return of the Spartans was an emotional and memorable day for Salida:

"The High School was in turmoil yesterday. Study was out of the question. School was dismissed, the band was called out, and the student body, bearing the team members on their shoulders, paraded through town, a happy crowd of Spartans."

At the beginning of the 1934 Salida High School season, the local paper announced: "Old King Football is about to climb on his throne in these parts of the hills and for several weeks such minor things as the FERA, the depression, and the rising cost of taxes will be lost in the excitement of watching the State Champions of last year meet what will unquestionably be hard competition for the next three months."

The Spartans kicked off the first game of the season against the Denver Rebels, a team that outweighed the Spartans on average 172 pounds to 150. It was of little consequence; they dispatched Denver 25-14. The following week, a squeaker against Colorado Springs, but Salida won 14-13.

A call to action was broadcast to SHS graduates at the end of October for the homecoming game. A parade was organized and "every class from the graduation class of 1890 to the present time is urged to have a car, bicycle, wheelbarrow, kiddy car or something to represent them in the parade."

School spirit payed off, along with some stellar football playing, and Salida handily whipped the Pueblo Central Wildcats 38-0. They steamrolled on, defeating Canon City 21-0, and then Pueblo Centennial 14-0, which again gave them the title of South Central League Champions. The legend of Coach White was beginning to form:

"It goes without saying that Coach White is the best known man in Salida, and he undoubtedly has done more single-handedly to put Salida on the map and on the tongue of sports fans throughout the West than any single person. The Salida team of 1934, like that of last year, has no outstanding stars – they play rather as a team. No one carries the ball all the time. The Spartans have a chance to have a state championship game played at home and if they do, it will reflect still further glory on that young man who has done so much to teach clean football in a way that wins – Coach Harold A. White."

The Spartans headed for Trinidad at the end of November to face the Miners in a semi-final showdown that would determine who went to State. As a special treat, the Denver & Rio Grande railroad commissioned a booster train for the Salida fans:

"The Spartans likely will be accompanied by a special train bearing 500-600 fans and the High School band. Coach White and the 22 players will leave Salida by car Wednesday for the southern city, while the special train will not leave Salida 'til early Thursday morning, arriving only shortly before the starting gun … The purple and white crew have tasted victory in 24 of their last 25 games, and have dropped only the Trinidad game in 1932 to mar a three year record."

It was a well-matched game but Salida beat out Trinidad 14-7, securing their place at the State Championships.

The excitement was palpable here, even more so because the Championship game of 1934 would be played here in Salida, the first time in the school's history. The heavy favorites were the Fort Collins Lambkins, a formidable team who had amassed a season total of 263 points to their opponents 7.

In preparation, the Salida High School field needed to be put in shape. New canvas fence was installed and the field freshly manicured. Tickets were printed, the school's glee club set up a concession stand, and the High School band made sure their instruments were tuned and ready for the big game.

With tickets selling for 75 cents ahead of the game and a dollar the day of, it was estimated that 2,000 fans would show up to the big game. It would be "the biggest classic Salida has ever witnessed." It was wryly noted that "Coach White will attend."

It was an epic game of defense. Each side held the other back until the last quarter when a Lambkin "attempted an end around play behind his own goal line and was smothered by more Spartan tacklers than he thought existed and was brought down." That safety was the only score of the game and Salida won 2-0 to retain their champion status. The Salida win shocked Fort Collins and the Front Range. Here was a team to be reckoned with:

"The Lambkins were tough, plenty tough, but they were not the equals of the Spartans. When a game moves along in one hour and 45 minutes there must be plenty of action and the fans agree, the action was there. Every second was fight, fight, fight, with the battle line swaying from one side of the center field to the other and rarely getting near the goal ... In the archives of Salida High it will be written that every man on the Spartan team did his best last Saturday."

The Board of Education declared a holiday and after a pep assembly at the school, pandemonium reigned in the streets of Salida. Like the year before, the entire student body paraded through town in celebration of their undefeated champions.

The 1935 school year began and the Spartans burst onto the season, first defeating Montrose 19-0 and then South Denver 34-0. Another week, another win:

"The Salida Spartans served notice that they are in the race for the 1935 South Central League pennant by running slip shod over the heavier Pueblo Centennial Bulldogs here Saturday 33-0."

In mid-October, the Spartans were set to play the Canon City Tigers and around 400 fans boarded the Denver & Rio Grande Special to see the game. They were in for a football fan's delight, a real nail-biter. The first half was uneventful but things took a turn in the second: "The Spartans 13-6 advantage was soon erased when Wilson of the Tigers crashed over the chalk line. The place kick teetered on the cross bar for ages and finally rolled fair to make the score 13-13 where it remained until the closing minute of the game when [Tuffy] Chambers skidded across the line end into pay soil carrying the oval safely tucked in his arms. In a game which nearly caused heart failure to the Salida fans on several occasions, the Salida Spartans emerged victors in the last minute of play to defeat the Canon City Tigers 19-13 in their annual classic played on Canon soil Friday afternoon."

The Spartans rolled on, terrorizing the Colorado Springs Terrors 38-0, scratching the Walsenburg Panthers 44-0, and savaging the Lamar Savages 16-12. This gave them the title of South Central League Champions for a fourth consecutive time. The Spartans were now set to face off in the State semi-finals in an away game against Wray.

Wray was worrisome: their field was made of sand rather than sod, which would be an advantage to the home team. The game was broadcast from Wray, and the play-by-play was transmitted live at the Empress Theatre here in town. The theatre was packed with those unlucky enough not to be able to get to the game:

"Salida was in danger several times. Wray plunged for big gains off tackle time and again. Wray made 15 first downs while Salida made five. [But] Wray's fumbles were costly. In the third quarter with the Spartans on their five yard line and their backs to the wall, Wray had only one yard to gain for a first down. Wray fumbled the ball. Wow! … In the last half of the last quarter something snapped into Salida and they began to show their championship stuff. They held Wray to three downs without material gain. Wray punted. Salida QB Gentile received it and away he goes ten, twenty, thirty, forty, fifty, sixty, and a TOUCHDOWN! The kick was no good. With only four minutes left to play Wray worked fast, but not fast enough. With five yards to go on the fourth down, Wray refused to kick and surrender the ball, but then failed to make the first down and Salida had the ball. [Star fullback] Oliver Brenton plunged through for the one yard gain and the timekeeper shot the game between the eyes. Salida was victor 6-0. It was a frenzied and frightened crowd until that touchdown."

The Spartans were undefeated and would face off against the Grand Junction Tigers for the State Championship. As usual, they were outweighed, the Junction boys averaging 170 pounds to the Spartans 151.

The Denver & Rio Grande special train was set to leave at 6 a.m. and the fans were ready. Denver & Rio Grande brakeman John Ritchie decorated the engine with festive purple and white streamers and then drew with chalk some Spartan heads on the wheels and the words "Coach White" and "Salida Spartans" on the front of the engine.

1935 Spartans

A crowd of 4,000 watched the game in Grand Junction where the Tigers fell before White's Squad 12-0. It was an easy victory. "All agreed that the Spartans outplayed the Western Slope lads in every department of the game and at no time during the game were the Tigers able to threaten the [Spartans]."

The Salida Spartans returned home on the D&RG Special, along with 500 of their fans, and the High School band.

One last time, the entire school closed up and everyone went parading with their Spartans around town. And these kids became legends in their own time. In four years, the Salida Spartans had won a remarkable 30 consecutive games. That year, three Spartans were named to the mythical '11,' the All-State-Team, a list of players selected by the sports writers of the Denver Post: Defensive End Stringari, Fullback Brenton, and Quarterback Gentile.

There are few moments in Salida history as magical as the 1933, 1934, and 1935 SHS football seasons. What would a person give to have been a witness to that history? The Denver & Rio Grande Special train to Grand Junction would have been a raucous celebration on the rails. To see the Spartans win the championship, and then return home with those conquering Spartans would have created a memory of a lifetime.

Thirty-Seven

A Spartan Tragedy

The Salida Spartans were the reigning champions of prep football in Colorado from 1933-1935. During the 1936 season, Coach Harold White and his Spartans won nearly every game they played due in large part to the talents of fullback and senior Oliver Brenton, the captain of the team. Unfortunately, they just missed out on winning the State Championship that year.

Four years after his arrival, Coach White had refined his team into a football powerhouse:

"Beginning with a scrubby squad in 1932, this man molded the small number of recruits at his command into championship material … The Salida Spartans were continuously losing their football games when Coach White happened on the field." But dedication and practice led to a phenomenal three seasons and "the climax came when the Spartans entered the finals for the state championship and won, then miracle of all miracles, they won and won again. It was Coach White who guided his small band to 39 victories."

In January of 1937, the unthinkable happened: Oliver Brenton was accidentally shot and killed by Coach White.

IN MEMORY OF
OLIVER S BRENTON
NOVEMBER 4 1916
JANUARY 9 1937

"ON HIM AND ON HIS HIGH ENDEAVOR
THE LIGHT OF PRAISE SHALL SHINE FOREVER"

The pair, along with Tuffy Chambers and Coach White's son, were rabbit hunting in the San Luis Valley and had come across an abandoned barn:

"Brenton entered the barn to stomp on the floor and chase the rabbits out, while White, with a .22 caliber rifle, and Chambers with a shotgun, waited outside. Coach White was firing under the barn. Evidently, Brenton got down on the floor of the barn and looked through a hole to see where the rabbits were huddled just as Coach White fired. When the stomping ceased, Coach White investigated. He found the boy lying with his head in the hole, unconscious and bleeding from a bullet wound over the right eye. The wounded boy was … rushed to the hospital in Salida. Chambers drove the car and Coach White held Brenton in his arms."

Oliver died en route to Salida.

The tragedy played out in real time as the information came out: "Coach White was so distraught he could not give the details of the accident. Chambers said he was 25 feet away from the barn and suspected nothing until he heard Coach White's screams after he had discovered the wounded boy … White was frantic with grief, and although powerful opiates were administered, he could not be put to sleep until 4 o'clock Sunday morning."

Oliver and Coach White's relationship was later memorialized: "Coach White and Brenton were like father and son. They hunted together frequently and were everyday companions. Coach White has always been a pal to all his football players but he regarded Brenton as one of the greatest football players ever produced in the United States with a brilliant college career ahead of him. Not only was Brenton a football player, but he was likewise a diligent student, ranking among the first division of his class. Colleges flooded him with offers. Although his high school football career ended after the Canon City game...Coach White did not stop teaching him, but kept diligently at it, giving the boy college football experience."

The death of Oliver sent shockwaves throughout Colorado's prep football scene. Denver Post sports writer Robert Gamzey eulogized Oliver Brenton:

"Brenton, greatest high school fullback ever developed in Colorado, and White, whose teams occupied the throne of state interscholastic football for three years ending last Thanksgiving Day, were at the very pinnacle of prep glory … Brenton died knowing only of victory. Never in four years of competition at Salida did he play in a losing game, never was Salida even tied … He was the best I ever saw in high school. From his fullback position he literally broke opposing lines in two with the crushing force of his plunges. He had a peculiar weaving stride, started like a bullet and was in full swing by the time he hit the line. It took three and four opposing players to bring him to earth, and time after time, he broke away when he apparently was stopped. In the open, he ran with speed and power, and more often than not, chose to bowl over tacklers in the open rather than sidestep them.

"He was a football player! After he manhandled prep teams that were the best in their section, Oliver was nicknamed 'Brute' and he never failed to live up to the name."

In the aftermath, Coach White recovered enough to keep teaching American History to his students at Salida High School but then resigned at the end of the semester and moved to Idaho, having secured a job as Director of Athletics at the Nampa High School. White later came back to Colorado and coached at Colorado College during the 1940s, though it never rivaled his success at Salida.

In 1977, Salida High School honored Coach White when they renamed the Spartan home field after him. It was an emotional meeting as most of the Salida Spartan champions from the 1933-35 winning seasons were there for the ceremony. White was presented with numerous accolades and every time a speaker lauded him "he received at least five straight minutes of applause."

Coach White died in 1978 and was buried in his hometown of Oskaloosa, Kansas.

Coach White's life shouldn't be defined by this tragedy. For a brief time in Salida's history, Coach White, Salida's Leonidas, along with his Spartans brought more joy to this town than it had ever known. If Oliver Brenton can be considered Colorado's greatest high school football star, it was due to Coach White's guidance and teaching. White rightfully may be considered Colorado's greatest football coach.

Endnote: At the beginning of the 1932 season, Coach Harold White wore a grey suit to the first game and the Spartans won. From that time forward, Coach White was always seen at Spartan games wearing the same grey suit. By the end of the 1936 season, this suit was in near tatters, and his assistants had to keep "a supply of blankets handy should the big fellow suddenly find himself out in the open here and there." But "the suit goes on or his boys won't."

In 1936, after the loss against Grand Junction for the State Championship title, Coach White retired his grey suit. It was cut into pieces and given to every member of the Spartan team: "Big Floyd (Tuffy) Chambers has one arm, Martin a leg, Haley the vest, Kochman a pocket, and so through the team the boys stripped their idol. Even [Frankie] Gentile, who is now playing with the Denver University team was mailed three buttons from that famous suit under which he fought never a losing battle."

Thirty-Eight

Salida Ski Train

In the fall of 1937, the Salida Ski Club was founded with the intent of promoting winter sports in the Salida area. To that end, they formed an alliance with the Denver & Rio Grande Western Railroad to organize a ski train.

At the time, the narrow gauge rails started across the river at the Denver & Rio Grande rail yards and ran over Marshall Pass to Gunnison. Today, the beginning of this abandoned rail line is the Monarch Spur trail. The Ski Club's plan was to work with the D&RGW Railroad and set up a cheap train service that would take skiers from Salida up to Marshall Pass. It was a great location and a great idea. The skiers could unload and ski down on the western slope side to the station of Shawano about four miles away and then an engine posted there would take skiers back up to the top of the pass.

That autumn, the U.S. Forest Service cleared out trees to make some nice runs come winter. In September, Frank Ashley, 'Denver winter playground expert,' went up with some locals to inspect the course. He deemed it "perfect."

A new position was created at the D&RGW to manage the ski trains. T.J. Flynn was appointed the 'Passenger Representative of Winter Sports.' In fact, T.J. was optimistic that at least one regular ski train could eventually be set up to run from Denver to Salida, and from there up to Marshall Pass.

A month prior to opening day, forty skiers took the train up on their own and enjoyed some fresh powder. It was a jolly group: "Aboard the narrow gauge on the trip up the pass, the group sang songs, accompanied by Horace Frantz, Jr. on his accordion."

With Salida humming in anticipation, the ski club chartered a train to Marshall Pass for the inaugural day. Among the events planned were skiing exhibitions and then a special treat: included in the 75 cent round trip train fare was a free visit to the Salida Hot Springs Pool. The pool had recently been constructed with W.P.A. (Works Progress Administration) money and was as yet unopened. Skiers could enjoy an après ski dip and make history at the same time, being the first to use the pool.

The big day was not just for skiers; it was to be a day for everyone: the president of the Salida Ski Club made an announcement in the local paper: "You do not have to be a skier to enjoy yourself on this trip. There will be tables for those who wish to play bridge and as the special train will be heated, those who don't ski can remain in the warm coaches and watch the others enjoy winter sports."

Gunnison heard about the Salida ski train and made plans to send their own train to the pass, $2 for a round trip ticket. A group of Puebloans was also due to arrive.

At 9 a.m. on Sunday, February 13th, the sold-out Denver & Rio Grande ski train special left Salida with over 400 people onboard. A baggage car held all of the skis and toboggans.

Once at the summit of Marshall Pass, the skiers disembarked and descended down the side of the pass to the little station of Shawano. It had been designated as a ski clubhouse for the day. The Gunnison delegation of over 150 skiers had arrived earlier that morning and enjoyed first tracks. The Pueblo delegation offered up 122, making it the largest group ever assembled on the Pass.

It was a beautiful bluebird Colorado day. Count Philippe de Pret, ski instructor at the Broadmoor and the nephew of the president of the International Olympic Games, initiated a ski school, giving out instruction to first-time skiers. There was also an exhibition ski race with ski racing champions Frank Ashley and Thor Groswold on a combination slalom/downhill course. Thor won the laurels of the day.

Frank Ashley and Thor Groswold

"Those who did not indulge in the winter sports enjoyed the spectacle of a whole mountainside filled with jumpers. A special car was set aside to take the skiers back up the mountain from Shawano, which is a feature no other ski course enjoys."

That evening when the train returned to Salida, a boisterous bunch of skiers stopped at the Salida Hot Springs Pool and celebrated until 10 o'clock that night.

Alas, the D&RGW's dream of a financial windfall from ski trains would not last.

In the summer of 1939, the new, modern Monarch Pass was constructed at a cost of 1.5 million dollars. It was the death knell for a potential ski resort at the top of Marshall Pass. Taking advantage of the new location, the Salida Ski Club, the U.S. Forest Service, and the W.P.A. got to work and in February of 1940, Monarch Ski Resort opened.

The D&RGW continued to take skiers up to Marshall Pass but it would never compare to that one magical day in 1938.

The Salida Ski Train only ran for two winters. After Monarch opened the D&RGW stopped the practice of picking skiers up at Shawano Station and toting them back up to the top of the pass. But they still operated a ski train of sorts. Bob Biglow, who grew up in Salida, remembered the fun times skiing up at Marshall Pass after its heyday:

"At the [Salida] depot on a Saturday morning, the train that went to Gunnison over Marshall Pass was dispatched and, in the caboose, would be several Salida people carrying their skis. We all got on that caboose at 6 in the morning. We took the train to the top of Marshall Pass, piled out … and there was a little bit of a depot there. We all gathered together and then took off skiing down the road that's somewhat parallel to the railroad track. The road continued all the way down to Mears Junction. That's where I learned how to ski. It was basically cross country, that sort of thing.

"Then, at Mears Junction, the train from Alamosa would show up at about 4 o'clock and bring us on down to Salida in the caboose again. It was a twelve-hour deal, 6 to 6. Just a delightful experience. I started [skiing] in about 1948 and then the train quit running about

1954. There were several years there that we did that. Just truly a great experience, which I totally, totally miss. It didn't cost anything, absolutely no cost involved. The railroad just gave anybody that wanted to go skiing a ride."

The Marshall Pass rail line was abandoned in 1953 and the tracks torn up in 1955.

Thirty-Nine

The Miracle of Television

In May of 1954, plans for a community antenna television system were presented to the Salida City Council. Salida was behind the times: across the country, network television programming had been airing for close to ten years. The mountains worked against us, hindering reception that other Americans living in the flats didn't have to contend with.

In July, City Council agreed to give a permit to the Salida TV Cable Company to build their TV antenna system.

500 feet south of Salida, a cable TV antenna was installed. In an editorial for the local paper, L.A. Barrett wrote: "Oddly enough, on the site chosen engineers have found that if they take a reading where the steel tower is located they get a good picture but if they take their trappings fifty feet or so in a northerly or southerly direction the strength of the signal decreases about half."

In preparation for presenting TV to the people, the Salida TV Cable Company held a dinner for over a dozen potential television dealers. They discussed how best to promote television in Salida. A visual demonstration was held at the new tower and all of the dealers viewed the quality of the picture coming through from the Front Range. W.K. Hooker of the Salida Electric Service said: "I would say that the picture is excellent, and of course the NBC network is one of the best programs on the air." The plan was to sell the idea to the public and then to begin wiring the city.

To that end, the local paper published an 8-page spread proclaiming the miracle of television. It was filled with advertisements and helpful articles entitled: 'What is Television? Here's How It Works' and 'TV Looks Better, Easier to See When Room Lights Are Left On' and 'Television Kitchen Helps Homemaker.' Most importantly, it was announced that public viewings of television would be held at the Salida High School gymnasium and auditorium at the end of October. Television sets and other prizes would be given away during the festivities.

Over 3,000 people attended the big TV event at the high school. Every television dealer in the region had on display their various makes and models which were hooked into a central cable system. As people progressed around the gym, they were able to see the same program on every set and compare quality. 2,000 people alone were on hand Friday night to see the opening ceremonies and to witness some local high schoolers who had traveled to Pueblo to perform at the affiliate KCSJ, which was then broadcast out to Salida and the rest of the region:

"All sorts and kinds of TV sets – table models, consoles, 17-inch screens, 21-inch screens, and even a giant 27-inch screen, were displayed by the local television dealers ... Some models were stripped down so the audience could see the internal workings of the sets. Tinkerers are advised not to bother the sets while in operation as electrical voltage is very high."

After witnessing this miracle of television, many Salidans commented "Look what we have been missing for all these years."

The Salida TV Cable Company newly renamed as Salida Community Television.

The sell worked and the process of wire installation began. It was $125 to get wire installed and hooked up to a house and then $4.50 a month for service with the Salida TV Cable Company.

In a record ten weeks, the entire town had been wired with 50,000 feet of coaxial cable. 200 homes had TV for Christmas that year.

Salidans started with just one channel, the NBC affiliate KCSJ, channel 5 in Pueblo and the signal was available for 10 hours every day from 11:30 a.m. to 10:30 p.m. There are those among us who are old enough to remember the sign off at the end of a broadcasting day; it was usually the station's identification, followed by the Star Spangled banner. Then the screen would go to static noise. When the set was turned off, the electrons that were emitting from the cathode ray tubes raced towards the center of the screen, creating a characteristic white dot referred to as a blip-out.

The following year, the Salida TV Cable Company renamed themselves Community Television Systems of Colorado. The company kept working to add other television channels. Due to our enclosed location it was becoming apparent that a new antenna was needed to pick up signals from the Front Range. In 1956, an antenna system was installed on top of Mt. Methodist. Lucky Salidans could now get a second television channel.

The next generation of TV system installation in Salida: Televents.

Forty

Chaffee County Opus

June Shaputis gave this county a great gift in 1987. She pored over the local newspapers to reconstruct a history of burials in Chaffee County and then put it all together in *Chaffee County, Colorado Burials*, her Chaffee County opus. This massive undertaking took her 25 years to compile, and is filled with the thousands of names of this county's deceased, dating back to 1860 and leading all the way up  to 1985. Along with these names, June included the location of the grave at the cemetery, or burial plot, and the date of the newspaper in which the deceased's obituary appeared. It is a researcher's gold mine, and empowers those of us working in the field of genealogy now and in future years to come.

Of the dozens of cemeteries located in Chaffee County, June additionally wrote a short history of each in her book. Most intriguing, she composed chapters on 'Unknown Burial Sites' and 'Outlying Graves' in the county.

Within June's opus, she will sometimes write 'good obit' after the date of an obituary. These are the interesting ones to look for.

In 1910, Herman Hentschell was found dead after falling from his prospect site in the Red Mountain district near Twin Lakes. He is buried in an outlying grave, near where his body was found. This is from his obit:

"Hentschell was alone in this world with no known relatives, but was well-liked through the mining section … The miners accompanying the coroner improvised a stretcher of small saplings and carried the lifeless form to camp. The body was prepared and tenderly laid away in the depths of the mountains and a huge stone rolled over the grave to mark the resting place and the end of the lone prospector."

What is an obituary? They are simple, small biographies of a person, meaningful to family & friends and to fellow townsfolk, and then helpful to the researcher. Some are poignant, and some are brutally honest. Judith Gill died here in 1901 "from the infirmities of her nearly four score years and ten in life's struggles. It was but the termination of a long, tedious journey." But an obit can also be so much more, a witness to a different time.

These are some of the people who June considered good obits:

John Jay, Sr. was born in 1870, and moved to Colorado from Iowa during the Leadville Gold Rush of 1879. His family settled in Maysville in 1880, which had just begun to boom due to the successes of the Monarch Mining District. He attended school there in the little red schoolhouse. "The hustle and bustle of those exciting days remained indelibly in his memory. In relating the events of his boyhood when visiting with his friends, he relived those rough and tumble years when the freight wagons loaded with ore and supplies for the miners crept over the narrow mountain roads, the crack of the driver's whip, and the tread of the miners boots over the board walks vibrated again and again in his ears. He referred to early day events as if they had occurred but yesterday."

George Pugh, who died in 1930, set the record straight on the correct history and spelling of Fooses creek drainage: "...It was named for one Foos, who intended to build a toll road through the gulch and over the pass to Gunnison but Hugh Boon and associates built Monarch Pass and the Foos route was abandoned."

Max Dickman, Salida's Justice of the Peace and police magistrate, died in 1945:

"In May 1860, Herman Dickman and wife Charlotte crossed the plains from Bloomington, Ill., to South Park, traveling in a covered wagon drawn by a spiked team and leading a milch cow. Max was born in Park County, about five miles from Fairplay on Aug. 27, 1860. The old timers informed the Dickmans that their son was the first white child born in what is now Park County." At his death, Max was believed to be "the oldest native-born citizen of Colorado."

Bob O'Haver was born in 1898, served in WWI, and worked most of his life in Salida in the oil business, at various times owning Shavano Oil Co. and working at Y&R Garage as a mechanic. He also served as a Chaffee County commissioner. In October 1948, Gray's Creek Reservoir was renamed O'Haver Lake "in honor of O'Haver's service in water and forest conservation."

Thomas Cameron, at one time the oldest settler in the valley, died in 1897. He first located to California Gulch at Leadville in 1860, then moved south:

"He took up the tract of land which has (since 1867) been his home, it being about the first ranch to be taken up in the valley. Cameron Mountain was named in honor of him and will forever stand as nature's monument to the man who was one of the few to crowd the red man farther into the mountains and pave the way for civilization."

And Tom Doyle, who died in 1948, alternated throughout his life between wealth and poverty:

"Death came this morning to one of the most picturesque prospectors in the history of mining in the Rocky Mountains. Tom Doyle had an instinctive knowledge of geology, which enabled him to find a mineral deposit. He made and spent several fortunes. He would often say that he knew what it meant to spend a million dollars because he had done it. ... When Cripple Creek was booming, Tom Doyle was there. When Leadville opened up, Tom Doyle was in the camp. He prospected in Aspen. His favorite haunt was the Paradox Valley in western Montrose County where he found enough rare minerals and precious metals to have made him one of the wealthiest men in the West, but money soon slipped from his grasp."

June wrote of her collection:

"I believe, rich or poor, famous or infamous, everyone's life is unique and everyone has a story to tell. Each person contributed to this area in some way, good or bad ... These burials did not just take place in cemeteries, but occurred on ranches, along roads, trails, streams and rivers, and sometimes beside a solitary miner's cabin."

And what of June's obit? She "haunted local cemeteries, investigated local ghost towns, and found great pleasure walking down shadowy dirt roads. She loved history and used to joke about collecting dead people. Over time she collected hundreds of epitaphs. One of her favorites was inscribed on the tombstone of a hypochondriac [that] stated, 'I told you I was sick.'"

That was a good obit.

Acknowledgments

Thank you:

Damon Lange
Paul Goetz
Susan Matthews
Jeff Donlan
Tuesday Evening Club
Vicki Bousquet and the Bradbury Family
Larry Kovacic
Chief Doug Bess
Chuck Rose

Gratitude to Donna Nevens for her encouragement.

To everyone who came up to the front desk and said they enjoyed an article, thank you. It was much appreciated.

Notes

Introduction

DENVER & RIO GRANDE RAILROAD COMPANY   Gordon Chappell, *Scenic Line of the World* (Colorado Rail Annual: 1970).

NEW SETTLEMENT TOWN   A member of the Tuesday Evening Club reminisced in 1897 about the tight-knittedness of brand new Salida: "In the early days of this camp, not so many years ago, when nails were at a premium, and most of us kept house in a dry goods box, the sociability of this town was a distinctive feature. Immediately after buying your first grocery bill you were called upon and made to feel at home. No one overlooked you. It was an unpardonable sin to neglect calling on each new victim as he struck camp..." (from "Salida — The Social Side," *Salida Mail*, March 23, 1897.)

NAMED BY GOV. HUNT   Richard Carroll, "The Founding of Salida," *Colorado Magazine*, vol. XI, no. 4 (July 1934): 121-133. Early settler Hugh Boon gave the credit of the naming of Salida to Gov. Hunt's wife. This is from his *Early Days in Chaffee County*, part of the Thomas Nevens papers: "When the present town of Salida was started in 1880, it was originally shown on the Denver & Rio Grand Railroad [maps] as South Arkansas. The name was not entirely satisfactory, since some confusion resulted from the fact that Poncha Springs was originally known as South Arkansas some years previous. Later the same year, Mrs. Hunt, the wife of Governor Hunt, vice president of the Denver & Rio Grande Railroad, was making a trip through this part of the country by train. She was gazing out of the car window as the trains emerged from the canyon below town and observing the beautiful valley opening up before her, she gave utterance to the Spanish word 'Salida' meaning 'outlet' or 'gateway.' It was seized upon as a fitting name for the town and the name was so changed ... However, at the time the Denver & Rio Grande Railroad had a large number of tickets printed up with the name as South Arkansas, which they continued to use until the supply was exhausted a year or two later. This was somewhat confusing to travelers since they would purchase a ticket to Salida and find they had one to South Arkansas and often think they had been tricked."

AGENTS MILLIE OHMERTZ   'Lots for Sale' advertisement, *Mountain Mail*, May 5, 1883.

WILLIAM VAN EVERY   Richard Carroll, "The Founding of Salida," *Colorado Magazine*, vol. XI, no. 4 (July 1934): 121-133.

SEVERAL STRUCTURE FIRES   Front Range Research Associates, Inc., *Downtown Salida Historic Buildings Survey, 2001-02: Final Report*, Denver, Colo., June 2003.

MOUNTAINS AROUND MONARCH   Henderson, Charles, *Mining in Colorado: A History of Discovery, Development, and Production*. Professional Paper 138. Washington, D.C.: Government Printing Office, 1926.

LAST PASSENGER TRAIN   "Special Car," *Mountain Mail*, December 8, 1964

OFFICIALLY, THE LAST TRAIN   Hunt, Chris, "No. 844 Steams Through Salida." *Mountain Mail*, June 23, 1997.

CHANGED SALIDA'S FATE   The July 1992 issue of Outside magazine ('Where to Live: Ten Towns That Have It All') hastened this along when they published a small blurb about Salida: "Be the first on your block to move to ... Salida, Colorado. Beef ranchers, intermediate and advanced Arkansas River whitewater paddlers, and deejays from KVRH (the WKRP of Colorado, on 1340 AM and 92.1 FM) coexist in the shadow of the 14,000-foot Saguache Range. Monarch Ski Resort, a state secret, is 20 miles to the west."

One - The Ute People

"ANTELOPE, BUFFALO, DEER, ELK" Fred B. Agee and Joseph M. Cuenin, "Indians," *History of the Cochetopa National Forest*, (Salida, Colorado, 1924).

"THE HIGH RIDGE" Ibid.

"THE UTES WERE A POWERFUL" Ibid.

ONCE THE SPANIARDS Southern Ute Indian Tribe, https://www.southernute-nsn.gov/history/chronology/

"THE SAVAGES WERE" Hubert Howe Bancroft, "The Extermination of the Indians," *Works by Hubert Howe Bancroft*, vol. 24, chapter XVIII, 474.

AROUND THE TIME Benjamin Madley, *An American Genocide: The United States and the California Indian Catastrophe, 1846-1873* (New Haven ; London : Yale University Press, 2017).

"THE INDIANS CLAIMED" Fred B. Agee and Joseph M. Cuenin, "Indians," *History of the Cochetopa National Forest*, (Salida, Colorado, 1924).

IN 1868 James Jefferson, Robert W. Delaney, and Gregory C. Thompson, *The Southern Utes: A Tribal History* (Ignacio, Colo.: Southern Ute Tribe, 1973).

WHITES RELENTLESSLY For one example of this the Pueblo newspaper, the Colorado Daily Chieftain, reprinted a column on January 22, 1880 from the New York World: The Utes "mean arson and murder and crimes against humanity ... we had better get the Utes out of the way of civilized people, and begin a new experiment at making the Utes something very different from what they are ..." The Fort Collins Courier from October 9, 1879, was more straightforward: "Powder and ball is the best Indian civilizer."

"THE UTE BILL" "The Ute Bill Passed," *Mountain Mail*, June 19, 1880.

"NOTWITHSTANDING SPORADIC OUTBREAKS"   Fred B. Agee and Joseph M. Cuenin, "Indians," *History of the Cochetopa National Forest*, (Salida, Colorado, 1924).

ARCHAEOLOGISTS HAVE RECENTLY   Michael Stearly, "Archaeological Heritage of Colorado's Ute Tribe: Part of National Forests' History in Rocky Mountain Region," (U.S. Forest Service, 2015) https://www.fs.usda.gov/features/archaeological-heritage-colorados-ute-tribe-part-national-forests-history-rocky-mountain.

Two - Hidden Treasure of the Spaniards

In its original publication, this article included a potential connection between this Spanish treasure map and the secret treasure that art dealer Forrest Fenn buried. Fenn's treasure has since been located in Wyoming.

SPANISH EXPLORATION WAS STILL   "A Tale of Buried Coin," *Herald Democrat*, February 11, 1898.

"BELOW WHERE BUENA VISTA"   "Buried Millions in Gold," *Salida Mail*, August 9, 1904.

"IT WAS A GRUESOME"   Ibid.

"THERE IS A MAN"   Ibid.

"THERE IS SOMETHING"   "Thomas A. Summers, Who Dreams of Buried Wealth," *Salida Record*, February 21, 1913.

"GUARDED BY HUMAN SKULLS"   Ibid.

"MEASUREMENT IS TAKEN"   "Spanish Treasure Located Near Salida," *Salida Mail*, October 8, 1912.

"WHERE HE WILL ATTEMPT"   "Treasure Seeker Back After Long Absence," *Salida Record*, December 5, 1913.

"EN UN VALLE"   *Salida Record*, May 28, 1937.

IN A ROUNDED VALLEY   Thanks to Bailey Escapule for this translation.

SEVERAL OTHER HIDDEN   Albert Proteau, "Some Facts and Fancies About the Early Days of Chaffee County," *Chaffee County Republican*, January 1, 1926.

Another version of this legend appeared in 1898 when a news report circulated of one Juan Garcia who claimed to be "on the track of a large fortune, supposed to have been buried near a big white cliff up the Arkansas River." ("A Tale of Buried Coin," *Herald Democrat*, Feb. 12, 1898) Garcia had been in the Spanish Navy and along with a friend, embezzled gold from their ship and traveled up the Arkansas River all the way to Mt. Princeton, where he went on to bury the gold. The treasure at this point was valued at $80,000. ("Cached in These Hills, *Chaffee County Republican*, Feb. 17, 1898)

Three - History of the Denver & Rio Grande Railroad

DENVER & RIO GRANDE   Gordon Chappell, *Scenic Line of the World* (Colorado Rail Annual: 1970).

"THE [D&RG'S] ARTICLES OF INCORPORATION"   Arthur Ridgway, "Denver & Rio Grande," *History of Colorado*, James H. Baker, editor and LeRoy R. Hafen, Ph.D., prepared under the supervision of the State Historical and Natural History Society of Colorado (Denver: Linderman Co., Inc. 1927).

IN 1871   Gordon Chappell, *Scenic Line of the World* (Colorado Rail Annual: 1970).

LOCAL JURISDICTION SIDED   Ibid.

"MOST OF THE BATTLE"   Ibid.

"EVERY PRACTICABLE CANON"   Arthur Ridgway, "Denver & Rio Grande," *History of Colorado*, James H. Baker, editor and LeRoy R. Hafen, Ph.D., prepared under the supervision of the State Historical and Natural History Society of Colorado (Denver: Linderman Co., Inc. 1927).

BY MAY 1   Richard Carroll, "The Founding of Salida," *Colorado Magazine*, vol. XI, no. 4 (July 1934): 121-133.

NATHROP HAD RAILS   Richard Chappell, "Scenic Line of the World," *Colorado Rail Annual*, 1970.

ABOUT 600 PEOPLE   Richard Carroll, "The Founding of Salida," *Colorado Magazine*, vol. XI, no. 4 (July 1934): 121-133.

"THE DENVER AND RIO GRANDE COMPANY"   "To Be Certainly Not," *Mountain Mail*, July 17, 1880.

BY 1886   "Why We Are Here," *Salida Mail*, December 31, 1886.

THE ROUNDHOUSE HELD   "A Railroad Center," *Salida Mail*, December 31, 1886.

THE HUB FOR SIX MAJOR   Front Range Research Associates, Inc., *Downtown Salida Historic Buildings Survey, 2001-02: Final Report*, Denver, Colo., June 2003.

"SOME PEOPLE LOOK"   "City Council," *Salida Mail*, April 19, 1892.

"IT WAS NOT"   "Gem of the Rockies," *Salida Mail*, August 12, 1892.

Four - The Batemans in Salida

HIS DAD, GEORGE   "George F. Bateman," *History of the Arkansas Valley, Colorado* (Chicago: O.L. Baskin and Co., Historical Publishers, 1881).

THE BATEMANS WERE ORIGINALLY   Fred L. Bateman, interview by Richard Carroll, transcript, Richard Carroll Collection, Salida Regional Library, Salida, Colorado.

"FATHER AND I"   Ibid.

"I WENT FROM PUEBLO"   Ibid.

"PONCHA SPRINGS, MAYSVILLE, GARFIELD"   "Fred Bateman's History of Salida," June 1934, Salida Regional Library, Salida, Colorado.

"WE HEARD THAT"   Fred L. Bateman, interview by Richard Carroll, transcript, Richard Carroll Collection, Salida Regional Library, Salida, Colorado.

GEORGE BATEMAN EVENTUALLY   Ibid.

"WHEN THE RAILROAD"   Ibid.

BICYCLE CLUB   See Salida's Wheelmen, chapter twenty-one.

Five - A Trip to Gothic

IN THE SPRING   Carl L. Haase, "Gothic, Colorado: City of Silver Wires," *Colorado Magazine*, vol. 51, no. 4, (Denver, Colo.: State Historical Society of Colorado, 1974) 294-316.

"THERE IS AT PRESENT"   "Gothic City," *Saguache Chronicle*, July 5, 1879.

ONE LOCAL REPORTED   C.E. Hagie, "Gunnison in Early Days," *Colorado Magazine*, vol. 8, no. 4, (Denver, Colo.: State Historical Society of Colorado, July 1931) 121-129.

RACHEL KEPT A DIARY   All diary entries are taken from Rachel Bradbury's Diary, part of the Patricia Holton Bradbury Collection, Salida Regional Library, Salida, Colorado.

GRAND CANON OF THE ARKANSAS   i.e. the Royal Gorge and Big Horn Sheep Canyon.

COTCHTOP PASS   i.e. Cochetopa Pass, pronounced 'Coach-Tope'.

THERE WERE AROUND   Carl L. Haase, "Gothic, Colorado: City of Silver Wires," *Colorado Magazine*, vol. 51, no. 4, (Denver, Colo.: State Historical Society of Colorado, 1974) 294-316.

"THEY STARTED FROM"   Ibid., p. 305.

"THEY DREW UP BESIDE"   Robert L. Brown, "Tour of Ulysses S. Grant," *Brand Book 1969: Silver Anniversary Edition*, (Boulder, Colo.: Johnson Publishing Company, 1970).

ON AUGUST 5, 1880   "Gunnison Pioneers Recall Visit of President Grant," *Steamboat Pilot*, August 10, 1939.

Six - Salida's Fire Boys

"ALL THOSE WHO"   "Salida's Business Men and Their Direct Interest," *Mountain Mail*, January 15, 1881.

"ONE OF THE FINEST"   "The Firemen's Ball," *Mountain Mail*, February 25, 1882.

BY SEPTEMBER OF   "Hose Company Meeting," *Mountain Mail*, September 16, 1882.

"THE FIRE BOYS"   "The Fire," *Mountain Mail*, November 4, 1882.

"BOYS YOU HAVE"   Ibid.

BY JANUARY 1883   Sanborn Fire Insurance Map Collection, Boulder: University of Colorado, https://cudl.colorado.edu/luna/servlet/view/all/where/Salida?sort=city%2Cdate%2Csheet.

"THE CONVENIENT AND PRACTICAL"   "Hose Company No. 1," *Mountain Mail*, January 13, 1883.

"THE TERPSICHOREAN EXERCISES"   "Firemen's Turn-Out," *Mountain Mail*, January 6, 1883.

"THE LITTLE FIRE BELL"   "Last Night's Fire," *Mountain Mail*, January 20, 1883.

"SOME OF THE FIRE BOYS"   Ibid.

"IT IS WELL KNOWN"   "Hose Company Wants," *Mountain Mail*, September 22, 1883.

"THE FLAMES SPREAD"   "A Disastrous Fire," *Mountain Mail*, September 8, 1883.

MOST NEWS ARTICLES ATTRIBUTED   One example was headlined in the April 7, 1891 *Salida Mail*: "A Disastrous Fire: Five Places of Business Burned Out in the Heart of the City. Loss Estimated at $15,000. The Fire Thought to be the Work of an Incendiary."

TWO WERE NOTABLE   Front Range Research Associates, Inc., *Downtown Salida Historic Buildings Survey, 2001-02: Final Report*, Denver, Colo., June 2003.

"MRS. HANLEY HAS"   "Fire This Morning," *Salida Mail*, November 29, 1884.

IN NOVEMBER OF 1887   "Salida Town Council," *Salida Mail*, November 25, 1887.

OVER $600 OF   "W.S. O'Brien Hook and Ladder Co.," *Salida Mail*, March 4, 1887.

A SEPTEMBER 1889   "A Beneficial Blaze," *Salida Mail*, September 24, 1889.

IN MAY OF 1890   "Consumed in Flames," *Salida Mail*, May 6, 1890.

"PROVE A BLESSING"   Ibid.

"IT IS ALTOGETHER PROBABLE"   Ibid.

"WITHOUT ANY GOOD CAUSE"   "Disbandment of the Fire Department," *Salida Mail*, May 13, 1892.

"THE BOYS GOT HOTHEADED"   Ibid.

"HAD BEEN VERY SHABBILY"   "Special Council Meeting," *Salida Mail*, May 27, 1892.

RAISE OVER $300   Ibid.

"THE ADMIRATION OF EVERYBODY"   "How We Celebrated," *Salida Mail*, July 5, 1892.

COMPETED IN A HOSE RACE   Ibid.

BY 1900   Front Range Research Associates, Inc., *Downtown Salida Historic Buildings Survey*, Architectural Inventory Form Resource #5CF406.101. Historical Background for 124 E Street.

Seven - The Richest & Unluckiest Man in Town

PETER MULVANY EMIGRATED   "Death of Peter Mulvany," *Salida Mail*, November 28, 1899.

CORNER OF FIRST AND G   "Mulvany Will Move," *Mountain Mail*, June 19, 1880.

SALES EARNINGS FOR 1881   "Peter Mulvany," *Mountain Mail*, December 31, 1881.

THROUGHOUT THE DECADE   "Nothing on Wheels," *Salida Mail*, December 20, 1889.

IN MARCH 1886   "Peter Mulvany," *Salida Mail*, December 31, 1886.

IN 1887, MULVANY BOUGHT   "The Mulvany Block," *Salida Mail*, October 14, 1887.

DURING THIS TIME   "Death of Mrs. P. Mulvany," *Salida Mail*, November 18, 1887.

WROTE POETRY   The Donna Nevens Collection at the Salida Archive has a selection of Peter's poetry.

THE UNOPENED BUILDING   "$175,000! The Greatest Fire Salida Ever Saw," *Salida Mail*, January 6, 1888.

"THE GREATEST"   Ibid.

A FAULTY FIREPLUG   Ibid.

"TO THE PUBLIC"   "To the Public. Fire! Fire! Fire!," *Salida Mail*, January 6, 1888.

"PETER MULVANY IS CARRYING"   "Peter Mulvany," *Salida Mail*, January 13, 1888.

PETER HAD REMARRIED   "Married — In Pueblo," *Salida Mail*, November 20, 1888.

"NO BUSINESS MAN"   "An Old Landmark Gone," *Salida Mail*, November 22, 1889.

BY DECEMBER, PETER BUILT   "Peter Mulvany, Pioneer Grocer," *Salida Mail*, December 20, 1889.

PETER SUFFERED THROUGH   "Death of Peter Mulvany," *Salida Mail*, November 28, 1899 and "P.Mulvany," *Salida Mail*, December 25, 1891.

"SPINNING AROUND SALIDA"   "Peter Mulvany," *Salida Mail*, July 26, 1892.

HE OPENED A HOTEL   "Union Hotel," *Salida Mail*, August 4, 1896.

IN DECEMBER 1897   "A Destructive Fire," *Salida Mail*, December 7, 1897.

"IF YOU WANT"   "If you want," *Salida Mail*, January 4, 1898.

Eight - The Capital Contest

"THE CAPITAL OF THE STATE"   "Where the Capital Should Be," *Mountain Mail*, May 7, 1881.

"TAKE A MAP"   Ibid.

"THE DIFFERENCE BETWEEN"   "The State Capital," *Mountain Mail*, September 10, 1881.

"DENVER'S UNEASINESS"   *Mountain Mail*, October 8, 1881.

"PUEBLO BASES HER CLAIM"   "The State Capital," *Mountain Mail*, September 10, 1881.

"THE [CANON CITY] REPORTER"   "Salida Land Grabbers," *Mountain Mail*, October 1, 1881.

"THERE IS PROBABLY"   "The State Capital," *Mountain Mail*, September 10, 1881.

ON NOVEMBER 8   Jerome C. Smiley, *History of Denver* (Denver : Old Americana, 1978).

"SALIDA DIDN'T CARE"   "The Capital Contest," *Mountain Mail*, November 12, 1881.

Nine - Rise of the Cattle Thieves

IN THE SPRING OF 1883   "Chasing Cattle Thieves," *Mountain Mail*, April 28, 1883.

IN NOVEMBER OF 1880   *Mountain Mail*, November 13, 1880.

A YEAR LATER   *Mountain Mail*, October 21, 1881.

TWO WEEKS INTO   *Mountain Mail*, November 12, 1881.

MONTHLY SALARY OF   "Town Board Proceedings," *Mountain Mail*, June 10, 1882.

CONCEALED WEAPONS WERE   *Mountain Mail*, July 29, 1882.

GUNS WERE RELATIVELY EXPENSIVE   National Park Service: https://www.nps.gov/common/uploads/teachers/lessonplans/1870CatalogueofGoods.pdf

"BAXTER STINGLEY, TOWN MARSHAL"   *Mountain Mail*, July 29, 1882.

"THERE ARE PERSONS"   "Murder Most Foul," *Mountain Mail*, June 2, 1883.

"I'D LIKE TO SEE"   Ibid.

A MONTH EARLIER   Ibid.

"HOLE OF INIQUITY"   *Mountain Mail*, June 9, 1883.

"NINEMIRE STARTED UP"   "Murder Most Foul," *Mountain Mail*, June 2, 1883.

"IN BUSINESS, HIS WORD"   "James H. Bathurst," *Mountain Mail*, June 9, 1883.

NINEMIRE WAS CONVICTED   "Broke Jail," *Buena Vista Democrat*, January 31, 1884.

HE WAS NEVER RECAPTURED   The Mountain Mail, February 23, 1884, reported that Ninemire visited his mother after his escape and proclaimed to her: "They may capture the others, but they will never take me alive!"

Ten - The Lynching of Lauren 'Ed' Watkins

"THIS WEEK THE COMMUNITIES"   "Cattle Thieves," *Mountain Mail*,
July 14, 1883.
BEEVES   Plural of beef, i.e. cattle.
DURING THIS TIME   "$1,000 Reward," *Mountain Mail*, August 25,
1883.
WATKINS HELD ROUNDUPS   "Obituary," *Mountain Mail*, August 18,
1883.
HE DID GOOD BUSINESS   George G. Everett and Dr. Wendell F.
Hutchinson, "The Ed Watkins Story (John Hyssong's Version),"
Under the Angel of Shavano (Denver: Golden Bell Press, 1963).
"WATKINS WAS 29"   Ibid.
AND AMONG HIS KNOWN   Ibid.
WATKINS SHOWED THEM   "A Statement," *Mountain Mail*, August
11, 1883.
"THE CATTLE TAKEN"   Ibid.   Replevin is a procedure whereby
seized goods may be provisionally restored to their owner pending
the outcome of an action to determine the rights of the parties
concerned (Oxford University Press).
"THE NIGHT WAS EXTREMELY DARK"   "Canon's Disgrace,"
Mountain Mail, August 18, 1883.
"THIS REVEALS THE ACT"   *Mountain Mail*, August 15, 1883.
"JUDGE GARRISON WAS CALLED"   *Mountain Mail*, August 15, 1883.
THE RANCHERS MADE IT   George G. Everett and Dr. Wendell F.
Hutchinson, "The Ed Watkins Story (John Hyssong's Version),"
Under the Angel of Shavano (Denver: Golden Bell Press, 1963).
THINGS COULD HAVE GONE   "That Lynching," *Mountain Mail*,
September 1, 1883.
THE CHARGES AGAINST   George G. Everett and Dr. Wendell F.
Hutchinson, "The Ed Watkins Story (John Hyssong's Version),"
Under the Angel of Shavano (Denver: Golden Bell Press, 1963).
"THERE HAS EXISTED"   "That Lynching," *Mountain Mail*, September
1, 1883.

"IT IS TO BE REGRETTED"   Ibid.

Eleven - The Murder of Baxter Stingley

"BAXTER STINGLEY WISHES"   *Mountain Mail*, September 29, 1883.
"ARMED TO THE TEETH"   "A Daring Act," *Mountain Mail*,
September 15, 1883.
SINCE CARRYING A CONCEALED   *Mountain Mail*, July 29, 1882.
"KNOWING JAMISON AND REED"   "A Daring Act," *Mountain Mail*,
September 15, 1883.
"NEVER BE TAKEN ALIVE"   "Brave Baxter," *Mountain Mail*,
November 3, 1883.
"SALIDA HAS BEEN INFESTED"   *Mountain Mail*, October 13, 1883.
"FRANK, I HAVE A WARRANT"   "Brave Baxter," *Mountain Mail*,
November 3, 1883.
"QUICK AS LIGHTNING"   Ibid.
"BOOTS WERE FILLED"   Ibid.
"THE VERY ATMOSPHERE TODAY"   "Baxter Stingley," *Mountain
Mail*, November 3, 1883.
"COMMITTING SUICIDE"   "Salida's Days of Blood Recalled by
Pioneer Who Witnessed Killings," *Salida Daily Mail*, December 16,
1939.
"TO BE PAID TO"   "The City's Action," *Mountain Mail*, November 3,
1883.
EVENTUALLY, $3,500 IN TOTAL   *Salida Mail*, August 9, 1884.
IN LATER YEARS, REED   Frank Reed was documented in the
following locations: Arizona - *Salida Mail*, August 9, 1884. Indiana &
Texas - "Frank Reed Located," *Salida Mail*, January 24, 1893. Illinois -
Salida Mail, August 9, 1884. Colorado - *Salida Mail*, February 9, 1884.
The City of Salida later resolved to withdraw the reward money for
the capture of Frank Reed; see the *Salida Mail*, May 6, 1887.
BAXTER STINGLEY HAD   "Fred Bateman's History of Salida," June
1934, Salida Regional Library, Salida, Colorado.

"PROPERTY WAS CAPABLE"   "Gold in an Old Cemetery," *Salida Mail*, March 13, 1894.

Twelve - Charles Rush's Memories of Leadville

"I DOUBT VERY MUCH"   All of Charles Rush's quotes and historical references come from his manuscript, *Memories of Leadville and Vicinity*, part of the Salida Regional Library's collection.
THERE WERE AN ESTIMATED   R.G. Dill, "History of Lake County," *History of the Arkansas Valley, Colorado* (Chicago : O.L. Baskin & Co., 1881).
THE POPULATION WAS AT   "City of Leadville," https://www.colorado.gov/pacific/leadville

Thirteen - The Cochetopa Forest

UTE FOR 'LITTLE ISLAND'   United States Department of Agriculture: Forest Service, "Vacation Trips in the Cochetopa National Forest" (1919).
PARCELED UP TO BECOME   Forest History Society, "The National Forests of the United States," https://foresthistory.org/
THE BOOM OF RAILROAD   Dr. Mike Eckhoff, Colorado State University, powerpoint presentation, author's collection.
"WOOD CHOPPERS, KILN FILLERS"   Charles Rush, *Memories of Leadville and Vicinity*, Salida Regional Library, Salida, Colorado.
"ABOUT 1880, FOLLOWING"   Fred B. Agee and Joseph M. Cuenin, *History of the Cochetopa National Forest* (Salida, Colorado, 1924).
"BUILT OUT OF BRICK"   Charles Rush, *Memories of Leadville and Vicinity*, Salida Regional Library, Salida, Colorado.
"RAILWAY BUILDING IN THE"   Edgar T. Ensign, "A Plea for Rocky Mountain Forests," Proceedings of the American Forestry Congress at Its Meeting Held at Atlanta, Ga., December, 1888 (Washington: Gibson Bros., Printers and Bookbinders, 1889).

THE EPA'S SMELTERTOWN REPORT   United States. Environmental
Protection Agency. Region 8 (Denver, Colorado), *Smeltertown
Superfund Site: Third Five Year Review, Chaffee County, Salida, CO*
(Denver CO : U.S. EPA, 2015).

Fourteen - Granite's Early Days

"ADVENTUROUS SPIRITS"   R.G. Dill, "History of Lake County,"
History of the Arkansas Valley, Colorado (Chicago: O.L. Baskin & Co.,
1881). A detailed account of the first discoveries of gold can be found
in *Mining in Colorado: A History of Discovery, Development, and
Production* by Charles Henderson (Washington, D.C., Government
Printing Office, 1926).
"INFLAMING THE IMAGINATIONS"   Ibid.
WAS CONSIDERABLY LARGER   Henderson, Charles W., "Figure 1 -
Map Showing Original 17 Counties Created in 1861 by First
Territorial Legislature of Colorado," *Mining in Colorado: A History of
Discovery, Development, and Production*. Professional Paper 138.
Washington, D.C.: Government Printing Office, 1926.
"THE EXCITEMENT THAT FOLLOWED"   R.G. Dill, "Leadville — Its
Discovery and Early History: History of Lake County," *History of the
Arkansas Valley, Colorado* (Chicago: O.L. Baskin & Co., 1881).
IT SOON HAD   E.R. Emerson, "History of Chaffee County: Cache
Creek," *History of the Arkansas Valley, Colorado* (Chicago: O.L. Baskin
& Co., 1881).
SEVERAL MORE VEINS WERE   E.R. Emerson, "History of Chaffee
County: Granite," *History of the Arkansas Valley, Colorado* (Chicago:
O.L. Baskin & Co., 1881).
BY 1900, MILLIONS OF   "Granite Has Good Strike," *Herald Democrat*,
January 23, 1908.
ORIGINALLY FROM ILLINOIS   "Bradbury Funeral Tuesday
Morning," *Salida Daily Mail-Record*, Oct. 31, 1956.

BY 1900, FRANK HAD   "The Bradbury Family," transcript, Patricia Bradbury Holton Collection, Salida Regional Library, Salida, Colorado.

"A REMARKABLE FEATURE OF"   "Granite Has Good Strike," *Herald Democrat*, January 23, 1908.

Fifteen - Ghosts of the Alpine Tunnel

IN JANUARY OF 1880   Lacy Humbeutel, "Tunnel for Sale," *Pueblo Star-Journal and Sunday Chieftain*, September 4, 1966.

BY AUGUST, THE DSP&P   *Elk Mountain Pilot*, August 26, 1880.

"THE ROCKIES PIERCED"   "The Rockies Pierced. Daylight Breaks Through the D.&S.P. Railway Tunnel," *Gunnison Daily News-Democrat*, July 27, 1881.

DSP&P SUPERINTENDENT OSBORNE'S   "The Alpine Tunnel," *Boulder News and Courier*, August 12, 1881.

HE WAS KILLED INSTANTLY   "Dennis McGuire, Of This City, Killed By Giant Powder in the Alpine Tunnel," *Leadville Weekly Herald*, July 9, 1881.

AND IN OCTOBER OF   "Leadville Laconics," *Leadville Daily Herald*, October 29, 1881.

ONE MAN SHOT AND KILLED   "Murder Near Pitkin," *Gunnison Daily News-Democrat*, July 27, 1881. "At Home," *Gunnison Daily News-Democrat*, October 29, 1881.

"A MOMENT LATER A GROUP"   "Paid in Full. Coleman's Debt to the Law Settled on the Gallows," *Gunnison Daily News-Democrat*, December 17, 1881.

"I'M GLAD OF THAT"   Ibid.

"THE SUSPENSE WAS AWFUL"   Ibid.

IT WAS GUNNISON'S FIRST   Ibid.

ESTIMATES VARY BUT IT   Dow Helmers, *Historic Alpine Tunnel* (Denver: Sage Books, 1963).

"THE SOUTH PARK BRANCH"   "Railroad Battle," *Leadville Daily Herald*, March 30, 1882.

"CHALK CREEK VALLEY"   Dow Helmers, *Historic Alpine Tunnel* (Denver: Sage Books, 1963). Reprinted from the *Denver Times*, July 15, 1882.

AT AN ALTITUDE OF   "Alpine Tunnel," *Mountain Mail*, August 12, 1882.

IT SPANNED OVER 1,700   "The Alpine Tunnel," *Boulder News and Courier*, August 12, 1881.

"ABOUT NOON ON WEDNESDAY"   "Denver and South Park Railway," *Elk Mountain Pilot*, July 20, 1882.

"THE DEPOT BUILDING"   "Disastrous Snow Slide," *Carbonate Chronicle*, March 15, 1884.

"I HAVE TAKEN COLD BATHS"   "A Terrible Trip," *Carbonate Chronicle*, January 3, 1885.

"I WAS FREQUENTLY INCLINED"   Ibid.

SNOW AND ROCK SLIDES   Dow Helmers, *Historic Alpine Tunnel* (Denver: Sage Books, 1963). The *Silver Cliff Rustler* reported on July 15, 1891 that "there is at present no prospect of Alpine Tunnel being opened on account of heavy rock slides and the great expense attending their removal."

"IN ITS CONSTRUCTION"   "A World's Wonder: The Alpine Tunnel One of the Greatest Engineering Feats of the Age," *Salida Mail*, June 25, 1895.

IN EARLY JUNE 1895   "Colorado Condensed," *New Castle News*, June 1, 1895 & "Alpine Tunnel Victims," *Salida Mail*, June 11, 1895.

LATER THAT JUNE   "Alpine Victims. Tragedy in the Big Tunnel," *Colorado Transcript*, June 12, 1895.

TRAINS RAN UNTIL 1910   Lacy Humbeutel, "Tunnel for Sale," *Pueblo Star-Journal and Sunday Chieftain*, September 4, 1966.

Sixteen - Electric Salida

"THE INCANDESCENT LAMPS"   *Salida Mail*, December 9, 1887.

THE PROCESS HAD BEGUN   *Salida Mail*, April 1, 1887.

AN ORDINANCE WAS THEN   "An Ordinance," *Salida Mail*, May 6, 1887.

THE PLAN WAS TO   "The Electric Light," *Salida Mail*, May 6, 1887.

IN AUGUST, OFFICERS   "Our Electric Light," *Salida Mail*, August 5, 1887.

A 75-FOOT SMOKE STACK   *Salida Mail*, October 28, 1887.

THE ORIGINAL 28 FT.   "The Edison Electric Light Company," *Salida Mail*, June 5, 1900.

"THE DINING ROOM OF"   *Salida Mail*, December 23, 1887.

"ALTHOUGH THE BEAUTIFUL"   Lacy Humbeutel, "The Monte Cristo Hotel: Salida's Famous Railroad Stop," *Humbeutel Diaries*, Salida Regional Library, Salida, Colorado.

PETER MULVANY'S HOTEL   "The Greatest Fire Salida Ever Saw," *Salida Mail*, January 6, 1888.

"THE ELECTRIC LIGHT COMPANY"   *Salida Mail*, January 6, 1888.

LATER THAT MONTH   *Salida Mail*, January 13, 1888.

"FROM DARKNESS TO TORCHES"   *Salida Mail*, December 2, 1887.

IN 1890, TWO NEW   "Furnishing More Light," *Salida Mail*, November 25, 1890.

A BRICK BUILDING REPLACED   "Fire Proof Building," *Salida Mail*, September 8, 1896.

EDISON COMPANY WAS SUFFERING   *Salida Mail*, February 10, 1905 & "An Ordinance," *Salida Mail*, April 18, 1905.

THE NEW COMPANY BUILT   "Auxiliary Plant Soon Completed," *Salida Record*, January 15, 1909.

"WHEN COMPLETED, THOSE DEPENDING"   *Salida Record*, January 25, 1907.

RESTICATE   Misspelling of rusticate, meaning "rustic."

Seventeen - E.D. Cowen, Newspaperman

GRAND TOUR OF EUROPE   Charles A. Murray, et al., *Newspaper Career of E.D. Cowen with Biographic Sketches* (Seattle: Western Printing Company, 1930).

"WAS THE ONLY NEWSPAPERMAN"   "A Brutal Assault," *Mountain Mail*, Sept. 15, 1883 & "Trial of C.C. Joy," *Carbonate Chronicle*, September 22, 1883. Charles Murray writes this of the attack: "For printing the truth, Mr. Cowen was the victim of a murderous attack in Leadville, from which he has ever since suffered and must continue to suffer the rest of his days."

"THE FRONT SEAT WAS"   "Alpine: A Stage Down the Valley, Ending at a Camp of the Most Brilliant Prospects," *Leadville Weekly Herald*, June 19, 1880. Also, typescript copies of all of Cowen's editorials are in the Donna Nevens Collection, Salida Regional Library, Salida, Colorado.

"WE HAVE AN ABUNDANCE"   Ibid.

"BLASTED HOPE"   Ibid.

"MINERAL OF CONSEQUENCE"   Ibid.

"NEW AND PROSPEROUS ASPECT"   Ibid.

BY 1880, DUE TO   "Maysville," *History of the Arkansas Valley, Colorado* (Chicago: O.L. Baskin & Co., 1881).

"AN OCCASIONAL INSIPID DRUNK"   "Maysville," *Leadville Daily Herald*, August 22, 1880.

HIES   i.e. to hasten

JOHN HUGHES WAS   "John H. Hughes," *History of the Arkansas Valley, Colorado* (Chicago: O.L. Baskin & Co., 1881).

"AFTER A FORENOON SPENT"   "Maysville," *Leadville Daily Herald*, August 22, 1880.

NICHOLAS CREEDE   "Retrospect: The First Settlers in the Monarch District," *Leadville Daily Herald*, August 28, 1880. See also Cy Warman's history of Nicholas Creede, *The Prospector: Story of the Life of Nicholas C. Creede*.

"THIRTY SUBSTANTIAL BUILDINGS"   M.V.B. McAleer, "Maysville. The Fourth at the Metropolis of Monarch District," *Leadville Weekly Herald*, July 17, 1880.

"FOR THE PAST"   "Maysville. The Fourth at the Metropolis of Monarch District," *Leadville Weekly Herald*, July 17, 1880.

SOME $420 MILLION   Henderson, Charles, "Figure 20 - Total Value of Gold, Silver, Copper, and Zinc Produced in Colorado from 1859 to 1922," *Mining in Colorado: A History of Discovery, Development, and Production*. Professional Paper 138. Washington, D.C.: Government Printing Office, 1926.

Eighteen - Mineral Wealth in Chaffee County

GOLD, SILVER, COPPER   *Salida Mail*, January 2, 1894.
"THE MARBLE DISCOVERIES"   "Colorado: Chaffee County," *Engineering and Mining Journal*, vol. XXXV: 369.
"THE NOTED ITALIAN MARBLE"   *Salida Mail*, September 12, 1890.
"H.L. ACKER HAS"   Ibid.
EXCAVATION HAD BEGUN   *Salida Mail*, April 5, 1895.
MUCH OF THE GRANITE   Wallace Moore and Lois Borland, "Quarrying the Granite for the State Capitol," *Colorado Magazine*, vol. XXIV, no. 2 (March 1947): 49-58.
THE MARBLE THAT WAS   "White Marble," *Avalanche Echo*, November 14, 1895.
ALSO FROM TAYLOR GULCH   "Chaffee County," *Silver Standard*, April 27, 1895.
"D.J. KELLY, CONTRACTOR"   *Salida Mail*, April 5, 1895.
THE MARBLE THAT REMAINED   R.D. Crawford, "Marble," *A Preliminary Report on the Geology of the Monarch Mining District, Chaffee County, Colorado* (1910): 69.
NELSON WAS AN AVID   *Salida Mail*, November 17, 1891.
REVEREND ROSELLE CROSS   Mark I. Jacobson, *Antero Aquamarines*, (Coeur D'Alene, ID: L.R. Ream Publishing, 1993).
IN 1887, HE FETCHED   *Salida Mail*, March 25, 1887.
"ONE CAN ASSUME THAT"   Mark I. Jacobson, *Antero Aquamarines*, (Coeur D'Alene, ID: L.R. Ream Publishing, 1993).
"GOOD BUSINESS AT THE TRAINS"   *Salida Mail*, March 20, 1888.
"GRANITE CENTER OF THE WORLD"   "Salida Growing as Granite Center," *Salida Mail*, October 9, 1908.

"THE SALIDA GRANITE COMPANY"   "Great Growing Granite
Works," *Salida Mail*, September 28, 1909.
CONCERN   i.e. company
"ITS STRENGTH FAR EXCEEDS"   Frank L. Hoenes, "The Granites of
Chaffee County, Colorado," *Mining Science Journal*, vol. 64 (July 13,
1911) 40.
THE MEMORIAL TO GOVERNOR   "Rose Pink Granite Wins National
Reputation," *Salida Mail*, 25th anniversary ed., 1935.
THE MORMON BATTALION   "The Mormon Battalion Monument,"
The Granite Cutters' Journal, vol. LI, no. 9.
BRINGING IN MILLIONS   "Rose Pink Granite Wins National
Reputation," *Salida Mail*, 25th anniversary ed., 1935.
"THERE IS NO GRANITE"   Ibid.
AROUND 75% OF THE HEADSTONES   Notes from Lewis & Glenn
Funeral Home, Salida, Colorado.
THE SALIDA GRANITE COMPANY   "Cornerstone of Library," *Salida
Mail*, May 8, 1908.

Nineteen - The Poet of the Rockies

'POET OF THE ROCKIES'   There are at least three references to Cy
being attributed this label: "Poet Cy Warman," *San Francisco Call*, vol.
74, no. 14 (June 14, 1893). "A Western Genius," *Salida Mail*, October
17, 1893. Nolie Mumey, "The 'Hogmaster' Poet of the Rockies,"
Denver Westerners Monthly Roundup, vol. 17 issue 5.
CY MOVED TO SALIDA   From the *Salida Mail*, April 4, 1885: "Cy
Warman is the future fireman of the 270, just from the shop, and is
happy, of course."
"ON THE SECOND DAY"   Nolie Mumey, "The 'Hogmaster' Poet of
the Rockies," *Denver Westerners Monthly Roundup*, vol. 17 issue 5.
CY WAS PROMOTED   Ibid.
"THE JOB OF FIREMAN"   Samuel A. Dougherty, *Railroad Tall Tales
(And Other B.S.)* (Grand Junction, CO: Printmasters, 1992).

HIS RUNS INCLUDED SALIDA   Nolie Mumey, "The 'Hogmaster' Poet of the Rockies," *Denver Westerners Monthly Roundup*, vol. 17 issue 5.

"I COULDN'T HELP WRITING"   *Current Literature: A Magazine of Record and Review*, vol. XIV, September-December 1893.

THE CANON OF THE GRAND   Cy Warman, *Mountain Melodies* (Denver, Colo.: Cy Warman, 1892).

"THE TRACK OVER MARSHALL PASS"   Nolie Mumey, "The 'Hogmaster' Poet of the Rockies," *Denver Westerners Monthly Roundup*, vol. 17 issue 5.

'THE PERPENDICULAR RAILROAD'   Cy's stories and poems can be found online at archive.org. 'The Perpendicular Railroad' is in *Short Rails* by Cy Warman (New York: Charles Scribner's Sons, 1900).

CY WAS FORCED TO   "A Western Genius," *Salida Mail*, October 17, 1893.

RENAMED WESTERN RAILWAY   "Cy Warman," *The Railroad Trainmen's Journal*, vol. VII (July 1890).

CY GOT A JOB   Nolie Mumey, "The 'Hogmaster' Poet of the Rockies," *Denver Westerners Monthly Roundup*, vol. 17 issue 5.

THE OTHER CREEDE NEWSPAPERS   *The Creede Candle* was Cy's biggest rival. In January 1892, Creede had four newspapers; six months later, there were a total of six. See *Colorado Newspapers: A History & Inventory, 1859-2000* by Jane C. Harper, et al.

CREEDE   Cy Warman, *Songs of Cy Warman*, (Boston: Rand Avery Co., 1911).

SELLING HIS PIECES   McClure's, The Century, and Harper's were three magazines that featured Cy's work. From Nolie Mumey, "The 'Hogmaster' Poet of the Rockies," *Denver Westerners Monthly Roundup*, vol. 17 issue 5.

ONE OF HIS POEMS   "Sweet Marie" (with music by Raymon Moore) was published in 1893.

WILL THE LIGHTS BE WHITE?   Cy Warman, *Songs of Cy Warman* (Boston: Rand Avery Co., 1911).

Twenty - Being Black in Salida

IN THE POST-CIVIL WAR ERA   For a history of Black people in Salida, most of the information I found was from the Mountain Mail, the Salida Mail, and the Salida Record at the Colorado Historic Newspaper Database. Also, the short essay "The Development of African American Newspapers in the American West, 1880-1914" by Gayle Berardi and Thomas Segady was a helpful resource in this writing.

THE PULLMAN PORTERS WERE   Denver & Rio Grande Railway advertisement, *Salida Mail*, October 23, 1888. Wealthy industrialist George Pullman manufactured the Pullman car which was a specialized sleeping car, noted for luxury.

THE PULLMAN COMPANY EXCLUSIVELY   Erin Blakemore, "Five Things to Know About Pullman Porters," *Smithsonian*, June 30, 2016, https://www.smithsonianmag.com/smart-news/five-things-know-about-pullman-porters-180959663/.

400 HOURS A MONTH   Jasmin K. Williams, "The Brotherhood of Sleeping Car Porters: The First Black Labor Union," *The New York Amsterdam News*, May 30-June 5, 2013.

"IT DIDN'T TAKE ME"   Malcolm X & Alex Haley, *The Autobiography of Malcolm X* (New York: Grove Press, 1965). Used with permission.

"NEGRO TENEMENTS"   New York: Sanborn Map Company, 1909.

NEWSPAPERS WOULD INTENTIONALLY   Gayle K. Bernardi and Thomas W. Segady, "The Development of African American Newspapers in the American West," *African Americans on the Western Frontier*, (Boulder, Colorado: University Press of Colorado, 2001).

"A GOOD SHARE"   "Colored Commotion," *Salida Mail*, March 4, 1910.

DEMIMONDE   From the French for 'half-world.' Here it is denoted to mean prostitution.

"MAYOR DUPAR AND"   "A Levee Clean-Up," *Salida Record*, November 8, 1901.

"THERE ARE TWO"   Ibid.

"BLACK MAN'S BURDEN"   "Black Man's Burden Greater in Salida," *Salida Mail*, December 18, 1906.

"YOUNG FAMILY, IN THEIR"   "George Wilson with Haverly's New Minstrels," *Salida Mail*, December 20, 1901.

"REALLY FUNNY COONS"   [Advertisement], *Salida Record*, November 10, 1899.

WHITE ACTORS BLACKENED   *Salida Mail*, February 3, 1899.

A RECIPE FOR 'BURNT CORK'   "Burnt Cork," *Salida Mail*, August 15, 1911.

"PROMINENT BUSINESS MEN"   "Elks in Black Face," *Salida Record*, June 14, 1907. The Elks were not alone in putting on minstrel shows. The Tuesday Evening Club (the Salida Library's founders) produced minstrels as well. Club member Martha Jones remembers: "We wore white canton flannel skirts, with fizzie side out, faces blacked, and wigs of black hair, the kind that is used in upholstered furniture. I was one of the end men and had a tambourine, I think my name was Dina Dewdrop. I also had the stuttering act. The interlocutor asked me the way to the Post Office, and when doing my best to stutter, to answer him (or her) purposely getting mixed up in my directions." (Tuesday Evening Club Collection, Salida Regional Library.) The minstrel show persisted; up into the 1960s, Salida High School and Longfellow Elementary both put on shows that featured students in blackface.

THE ONLY INFORMATION THAT   Gayle K. Berardi and Thomas W. Segady, "The Development of African American Newspapers in the American West, 1880-1914," *African Americans on the Western Frontier* (Boulder, Colorado: University Press of Colorado, 2001).

CHURCH WAS HOLDING SERVICES   "Church Notices and Notes," *Salida Mail*, March 26, 1909.

THAT WAS REPORTED   "Rio Grande Blockade Prevented by a Friend," *Salida Mail*, July 27, 1915.

"PEOPLE ARE NOT"   James Baldwin, *The Fire Next Time* (New York: Vintage International, 1991). Used with permission.

Twenty-One - Salida's Wheelmen

"TWELVE MEMBERS OF THE CLUB"   "Knee breeches," *Mountain Mail*, August 25, 1883.

ONE LONE BICYCLE OWNER   *Salida Mail*, January 19, 1884.

"SALIDA WILL HAVE"   *Salida Mail*, April 20, 1888.

"THE PONCHA BOULEVARD"   *Salida Mail*, May 8, 1888.

CITY COUNCIL SOON RESPONDED   *Salida Mail*, May 15, 1891. The Salida Wheel Club had requested of City Council a permit to ride their bicycles on the sidewalk "on account of the road being impassable for wheels," *Salida Mail*, May 10, 1895.

"WENT UP TO BUENA VISTA"   *Salida Mail*, April 28, 1891.

"BIKE SUITS"   *Salida Mail*, May 22, 1891.

CITY COUNCIL WAS ISSUING   *Salida Mail*, June 3, 1891.

"ECLIPSING ALL FORMER"   *Salida Mail*, June 21, 1892.

"IT MUST BE SAID"   "The Bicycle Race," *Salida Mail*, September 13, 1892.

"A NUMBER OF SALIDA'S"   *Salida Mail*, April 3, 1894.

SCORCHING   To ride a bike at an aggressively fast speed.

ON A SUNDAY MAY MORNING   *Salida Mail*, May 4, 1894.

"THE SUBJECT OF ORGANIZING"   *Salida Mail*, May 11, 1894.

"I LOOK OUT OF MY COUPE"   "The New Woman," *Salida Mail*, February 4, 1896.

"ALL CYCLISTS, WHETHER MEMBERS"   *Salida Mail*, May 29, 1894.

THE FIRST BIG BIKE RACE   "They're Off!," *Salida Mail*, August 16, 1895.

"THE FIRST TIME PRIZE"   "The Medal Prizes," *Salida Mail*, August 13, 1895.

"J.N. SIMMONS IS FOND"   *Salida Mail*, April 22, 1890.

"THE NUMBER OF BICYCLES"   *Salida Mail*, April 17, 1896.

DECORATION DAY   i.e. Memorial Day

"THE BAR REPRESENTS"   "The Road Race," *Salida Mail*, May 26, 1896.

"EVERY MAN, WOMAN, AND CHILD"   Ibid.

"EVERYONE MADE A GOOD START"   "Densmore Wins," *Salida Mail*, June 2, 1896.

"YORK RODE A TEMPLE"   "Notes on the Day," *Salida Mail*, June 2, 1896.

"THE GRAND PARADE OF WHEELMEN"   "Densmore Wins," *Salida Mail*, June 2, 1896.

"THIS REMARKABLE FEAT"   "Through in Fifteen Hours," *Salida Mail*, June 15, 1897.

"WE EXTEND TO YOU"   "Messages from the Mayors," *Salida Mail*, June 22, 1897.

THE WHEELMEN ESTIMATED   "A Sure Go," *Salida Mail*, August 7, 1896.

TO HELP RAISE MONEY   "The Wheelmen's Ball," *Salida Mail*, September 25, 1896.

FOOTBALL GAMES WERE LATER   *Salida Mail*, October 23, 1900.

"WHEELMEN'S ORGANIZATIONS HAVE CEASED"   "Salida Club Wheel Division," *Salida Mail*, May 14, 1897.

"BICYCLES ARE IN"   *Salida Mail*, January 17, 1896.

Twenty-Two - Vigilante Justice

HOLLIS D. SPENCER GOT A JOB   "Town Council," *Salida Mail*, January 6, 1891.

THE ITALIANS OVERTOOK BRILEY   "A Double Tragedy," *Salida Mail*, February 24, 1891.

"SULLIVAN … HAD WITNESSED"   Ibid.

SADDLE ROCK RESTAURANT   The Salida Mail's write up of the Briley/Sullivan incident refers to City Marshal McKelvey placing Briley under arrest in front of Comstock's restaurant. The Saddle Rock Restaurant was known as 'Comstock's,' after the owner, S.H. Comstock. The restaurant can be located on the 1890 Sanborn Fire Insurance maps. The Salida city directory for 1907-08 lists the 'Saddle Rock Rooms' at 131 Lower F.

EARLIER IN THE YEAR   "A Double Tragedy," *Salida Mail*, February 24, 1891 & "Funeral Held Today for H.D. Spencer, Pioneer Salidan," *Salida Daily Mail*, August 3, 1938. 117 W. 2nd was later home to Ideal Cleaners. It is no longer standing.

OLIVER BRILEY WAS LEG-CHAINED   "A Double Tragedy," Salida Mail, February 24, 1891.

"THE MOB PLACED"   Ibid.

HIS BODY HAD BEEN   "The Blackest Page," *Salida Mail*, June 5, 1900. This article also relates the brutality of the scene: "A mob surrounded the building and with difficulty the officers held the excited people back. Finally some turbulent and excitable men got in the rear of the building and began shooting through the building ... The guards were overpowered and soon a rope was around the unfortunate man's neck and he was jerked loose from the floor by dozens of furious men pulling on the rope. He was dragged into the street and an attempt was made to hang him to a light pole, but the rope was too short. The man was dead by this time, but the howling mob still dragged his body about and kicked and cuffed it and tried to find a place to hang it."

"A GROUP OF LYNCHERS"   "Funeral Held Today for H.D. Spencer, Pioneer Salidan," *Salida Daily Mail*, August 3, 1938. Hollis wrote in later years that the body of Oliver Briley was strung up at 1st and F Streets. This is contradictory to what was published in the local newspaper after the event. The railroad crossing was the Denver & Rio Grande Railroad's narrow gauge track that traveled towards Marshall Pass and beyond. The crossing was located at 1st and G Streets. It must be presumed that Hollis misremembered F for G Street.

IRON MIKE   19th century slang for statue.

"MOST OF THOSE"   "The Blackest Page," *Salida Mail*, June 5, 1900.

Twenty-Three - Disorderly Salida

A note regarding the spelling of Laura's last name, 'Evans' vs. 'Evens' - I adhere to the spelling 'Evans' which is how her name was spelled in the newspapers of the era, and the Salida city directories from the 1940s.

"I DIDN'T KNOW ANYTHING"   Laura Evans Tapes — Mazzulla Collection, Amon Carter Museum, tape #4, interview: 5/4/1951. Mss.01881, Fred Mazzulla manuscript collection, History Colorado.

"CHRISTIANSEN BJORNSON ARRIVED"   "He Lost $200," *Salida Mail*, January 22, 1897.

"ABOUT ALL THAT BJORNSON"   Ibid.

BETWEEN 1911 AND 1913   "Total Arrests Made by Salida Police Force April 1911 to April 1913," *Salida Record*, April 18, 1913.

AT LEAST THREE PROSTITUTES   Nora McCord and Dick Valentine were successful suicides. "Second Girl of Red Light Tries Death," *Salida Record*, October 24, 1913. Miss Blanche was unsuccessful. "Attempt at Suicide Made By Woman," *Salida Record*, July 18, 1913.

SALIDA'S 'MORALS COMMITTEE'   "Removal Redlight District in Sight," *Salida Mail*, June 13, 1913.

TOWN LEADERS AND CITIZENS   "Closing of Red Light District Under Advisement," *Salida Record*, June 6, 1913.

SOME COMMUNITY MEMBERS WERE AGAINST   "Mayor Alexander to Call Special Session of Council to Discuss Question," *Salida Record*, June 6, 1913.

"THIS SYSTEM HAS BEEN"   "Red Light District To Go Slowly," *Salida Record*, June 13, 1913.

A PLAN WAS ESTABLISHED TO REMOVE   "Social Problem for Careful Consideration," *Salida Record*, March 6, 1914.

LAURA KEPT HER BUSINESS   Jan MacKell, *Brothels, Bordellos, & Bad Girls: Prostitution in Colorado 1860-1930* (Albuquerque [NM] : University of New Mexico Press, 2004).

"SHOWING THAT THE CRIMINAL"   "Little Use for Jails in County or City," *Salida Record*, March 10, 1916.

IN 1916, SIXTY-THREE PEOPLE   "Arrests Decrease in Salida Under Prohibition Regime," *Salida Mail*, January 2, 1917.

SPECIALLY-LICENSED PHARMACIST   "Saloons Quit Before Midnight and Close Doors," *Salida Mail*, December 31, 1915.

MIKE CALVANO'S STILL   "Three Stills Seized in Salida; One Owner Fined, Others Jailed," *Salida Mail*, December 29, 1922.

OPEN DOOR POLICY   "Ex-Saloons," *Salida Mail*, January 11, 1916.

FRANK FILIPPONE   "Bootlegger Fined $100," *Salida Mail*, November 10, 1916

Twenty-Four - The Innkeeper and the Ambassador

MONTE CRISTO HOTEL   Front Range Research Associates, Inc., *Salida, Colorado Historic Buildings Survey, 2005-06: Final Survey Report* (Denver, Colo.).

CHARLES CATLIN MOVED TO   *Salida Mail*, March 24, 1899.

CHARLES INHERITED THE DOG   Duke died in 1902, just three years after Catlin arrived in Salida. It was common knowledge that Duke was 'for so many years a conspicuous landmark about the Monte Cristo hotel' (*Salida Mail*, January 6, 1903). It can be surmised that Duke was living in Salida before Charles Catlin began working at the hotel.

DINNERS WERE LUXURIOUS   *Salida Record*, April 5, 1901.

ONE NOVEMBER EVENING   "Mr. and Mrs. Catlin Entertain," *Salida Record*, November 6, 1903.

"ON WEDNESDAY THERE WERE"   *Salida Mail*, July 12, 1901.

"EVERYONE KNEW HIM"   "Dog Dead Twenty Years; His Monument Repaired," *Salida Mail*, October 4, 1921.

DUKE DIED   "Newspaper Man Visits Salida and Makes Favorable Comments," *Salida Mail*, February 6, 1903.

"WE GOT BACK IN TIME"   Ibid.

IN MEMORY OF DUKE   "To Mark Resting Place," *Salida Mail*, January 6, 1903.

THE MONTE CRISTO WAS SOLD   *Salida Mail*, January 26, 1904 and *Salida Record*, February 12, 1904.

CHARLES RETURNED TO SALIDA   "New Management for Hotel Denton," *Salida Mail*, November 22, 1910.

BUILT IN 1890   "Salida as Others See It," *Salida Mail*, March 14, 1890.

"MR. CATLIN CANNOT FAIL"   *Salida Mail*, April 7, 1911.

JUSTICE OF THE PEACE   "C.F. Catlin is Named J.P. by County Commissioner," *Salida Mail*, February 9, 1917.

"HE HAS BECOME SO"   "Judge C.F. Catlin Ties One Hundred Couples," *Salida Mail*, March 11, 1921.

IN !941, THE MONTE CRISTO   Front Range Research Associates, Inc., Salida, *Colorado Historic Buildings Survey, 2005-06: Final Survey Report* (Denver, Colo.).

Twenty-Five - The Footbridge

MILES MIX   "M. Mix, at the Mix House, *Mountain Mail*, January 29, 1881. Hugh Boon remembered Mix as being "a big stout fellow, somewhat of a bully, and usually made his bluff stick." (*Supplemental Statement by Hugh Boon*, May 12, 1924 by Fred B. Agee, Thomas Nevens Papers, Donna Nevens Collection.)

MIX BUILT THE BRIDGE   *Mountain Mail*, September 24, 1881.

SPECIAL COMMITTEE FORMED   *Salida Mail*, July 3, 1888.

IN 1899, A DAM BROKE   *Salida Mail*, June 20, 1899.

"CONSIDERABLE EXCITEMENT WAS CAUSED"   Ibid.

IN 1904, THE GRAND ARMY   *Salida Mail*, May 20, 1904.

"IMMEDIATELY AT THE CLOSE"   Ibid.

OVER A THOUSAND PEOPLE   "Swept to Death in Raging Flood," *Salida Record*, June 3, 1904.

"IT MIGHT HAVE BEEN"   "Brief History of the Great Memorial Day Disaster," *Salida Mail*, June 7, 1904.

THE BRIDGE HAD BEEN KNOWN   "Monday's Catastrophe," *Salida Record*, June 3, 1904.

R.A. HOLLAND, CHARLES LINES   *Salida Record*, February 24, 1905.

THE CITY WAS FOUND   "The Foot Bridge Verdict," *Salida Mail*, July 28, 1905.

INSTIGATED THE REPLACEMENT   Front Range Research Associates, Inc., *Downtown Salida Historic Buildings Survey 2001-02*, Architectural Inventory Form Resource # 5CF406.75. Historical background for F St. Bridge.

A NEW CABLE BRIDGE   *Salida Record*, July 29, 1904.

THE NEW BRIDGE   "Off the Fatal Foot Bridge Into the Surging River," *Salida Mail*, February 21, 1905.

Twenty-Six - Salida's Music Teacher

RAMEY WAS A SELF-TAUGHT   "James S. Ramey," *Salida Mail*, June 5, 1900.

AT THE CHICAGO CONSERVATORY   "J.S. Ramey, Prominent Salidan, Dead; Councilman and Talented Musician," *Salida Mail*, November 13, 1934.

THE GROUP'S EARLY ATTENDANCE   *Salida Mail*, August 7, 1891.

"PROFESSOR RAMEY HAS QUITE"   *Salida Mail*, January 24, 1893.

HE MARRIED KITTY   "Ramey-Jay," *Salida Mail*, April 26, 1895.

RAMEYS MOVED INTO A HOUSE   *Salida Mail*, May 13, 1898.

ONE OF HIS FIRST COMPOSITIONS   "Editorial Comment," *Salida Mail*, March 25, 1892.

JAMES RAMEY'S JUVENILE ORCHESTRA   "The Phantasma Draws a Good Audience and Presents Many Pretty Features in Drills and Representations," *Salida Mail*, October 10, 1899.

"BEST MUSIC THE RAMEY BOYS"   "Comment Upon Happenings and Doings at Maysville," *Salida Mail*, April 29, 1902.

THE RAMEY ORCHESTRA PERFORMED   "A Gala Day at Howard," *Salida Mail*, July 8, 1904.

THE METHODIST CHURCH HELD   "Ten Nights in a Barroom," *Salida Mail*, February 3, 1905.

PREVIOUS YEAR SELLING ALCOHOL   1904 Compiled Ordinances of the City of Salida, ordinance 238, section 11, Donna Nevens Collection, Salida Regional Library, Salida, Colorado.

REGULARLY DROVE THEIR DOCTRINE   There are numerous articles regarding the activities of the Women's Christian Temperance Union from this time period in the Salida Mail and Salida Record.

"WHERE LEWD PERSONS ASSEMBLE"   1904 Compiled Ordinances of the City of Salida, ordinance 220, section 13, Donna Nevens Collection, Salida Regional Library, Salida, Colorado.

"IT IS SAID THAT"   J.S. Ramey, "Short Music Talks: History, Biography, Theory, Harmony and General Comments," *Salida Mail*, April 27, 1928.

LOW   i.e. inferior

JAMES RAN FOR CITY COUNCIL   "James S. Ramey," *Salida Mail*, June 5, 1900.

CONTROVERSIAL IN THAT   "Ramey's Song Is Urged as New Colorado Melody," *Salida Mail*, January 23, 1917.

REPRESENTATIVE A.E. WRIGHT INTRODUCED   "Ramey's Ballad Subject of Bill in Legislature," *Salida Mail*, January 26, 1917.

BOTH THE COLORADO SENATE   *Salida Mail*, February 27, 1917.

"THE PARALLEL MAJOR AND MINOR"   J.S. Ramey, "Short Music Talks: History, Biography, Theory, Harmony and General Comments," *Salida Mail*, April 24, 1928.

"I TRUST THAT I HAVE"   Ibid.

"FREQUENTLY, I AM ASKED"   J.S. Ramey, "Short Music Talks: History, Biography, Theory, Harmony and General Comments," *Salida Mail*, June 15, 1928.

"THE CITY COUNCIL LAST NIGHT"   "City Council Adopts Ordinance to Prohibit Music in Taverns," *Salida Daily Mail*, June 7, 1938.

Twenty-Seven - The Tenderfoot Magazine

"THE SUCCESS OF THE TENDERFOOT"   "School Notes," *Salida Mail*, January 21, 1910.

"THE SALIDA BASKETBALL GIRLS"   "Girls' Basketball," *The Tenderfoot*, May 1910, 39.

"ONCE UPON A TIME"   "New Yells," *The Tenderfoot*, December 1909, 14.

"MR. DIVERS AND ARTHUR FRENCH"   "Young Men Building Wireless," *Salida Mail*, Oct. 25, 1912.

OMER WENT ON TO   Information from Omer Divers, Jr., email correspondence to author, July 2017.

THE CRATER   A geologic formation in the shape of a natural amphitheater in the Arkansas Hills northeast of Salida. The first mention of the Crater may have appeared in the Mountain Mail issue, dated October 15, 1881: "There are many beautiful spots in the mountains near town that the people know nothing about. Last Sunday, a crowd of about a dozen persons were up in the hills west of Cleora, and, first thing they knew, they were standing on the brink of a hill looking down into a regular amphitheater, in which were monuments of very peculiar formation, gulches and caves that are really wonderful. The place is well worth a visit."

"REMEMBER THAT THE GREATER PART"   "The End and the Beginning," *The Tenderfoot*, May 1911, 15.

"WHY DID WE SURVIVE?"   "Why We Survive," *Le Resume*, 1915, 62.

LE RESUME, NAMED BY   "Contest Name for Annual," *Le Resume*, 1913, 4.

"AN ARABIAN LEGEND TELLS"   "An Appreciation," *Le Resume*, 1913, 7.

Twenty-Eight - It Is Worthwhile

"FROM THE START WE"   Eighth Annual Convention of the South Central District, Salida, Colorado, (May 17, 1932), Salida Regional Library, Salida, Colorado.

'OPERAE PRETIUM EST'   Shorter Latin translation: It is worthwhile.
Longer Latin translation: The work is worthwhile.

"I WENT TO DENVER"   Letter from Mary Ridgway to the Tuesday
Evening Club, September 20, 1934, Salida Regional Library, Salida,
Colorado.

THE SALIDA LIBRARY ASSOCIATION   "Library Incorporated," *Salida
Mail*, August 26, 1902.

THE COLLECTION WAS THEN MOVED   F.W. Gloyd, "History &
Growth of Salida Public Library." Speech given at Rotary Club,
Salida, Colorado, January 22, 1951, Salida Regional Library, Salida,
Colorado.

THEY SPONSORED LECTURES   The Tuesday Evening Club's
entertainments were frequently written up in the local papers. The
Salida Record's article "New Library Formally Opened" (dated May
14, 1909) included the following paragraph: "It is thirteen years since
the first books were purchased as a nucleus for this public library,
and a retrospect of the work to raise funds during that time brings
kaleidoscopic visions of home talent plays, a Dickens entertainment,
Lady Minstrels, suppers, picnics, entertainment courses,
subscriptious papers, and a host of other money-making devices."

THEY EVEN HELD   "The Passion Play" and "Local News Notes,"
Salida Mail, December 3, 1907.

"SALIDA WANTS SOME OF"   *Salida Mail*, July 21, 1905.

"IF THE CITY AGREES"   Letter from Jas. Bertram to Ruth Spray,
dated December 23, 1905, Salida Regional Library, Salida, Colorado.

MARY RIDGWAY AND HER HUSBAND   F.W. Gloyd, "History and
Growth of Salida Public Library." Speech given at Rotary Club,
Salida, Colorado, January 22, 1951, Salida Regional Library, Salida,
Colorado.

THE CORNERSTONE OF SALIDA   "Cornerstone of Library," *Salida
Mail*, May 8, 1908.

"THE SPEECHES WERE ALL"   Ibid.

A BOX WAS PLACED WITHIN   Ibid.

BUILT AT A COST   Tuesday Evening Club manuscript from the
Noranne Giemer Collection, Salida Regional Library, Salida,
Colorado.

THE CLUB IMMEDIATELY HANDED   "City Council Accepts Library,"
Salida Record, February 5, 1909.

A DEDICATION WAS HELD   "Carnegie Library Formally Opened,"
Salida Mail, May 11, 1909.

"IT SHALL BE UNLAWFUL"   1904 Compiled Ordinances of the City
of Salida, ordinance 238, section 11, Donna Nevens Collection, Salida
Regional Library, Salida, Colorado.

AT ONE OF THE CHAUTAUQUAS   Incidentally, this was held at
Chautauqua Park which was a ½ mile down from F Street on W. 2nd
Street.

"WHETHER WE APPROVE"   "Chautauqua Closes With Big
Attendance," *Salida Mail*, July 28, 1908.

"WE ARE STILL"   Daniel Dorchester, *The Liquor Problem in All Ages*.
New York: Phillips & Hunt, 1884.

Twenty-Nine - Salida Red Cross

THE TUESDAY EVENING CLUB   "Tuesday Evening Club Organizing
a Red Cross Chapter," *Salida Mail*, March 27, 1917.

THE FIRST ORGANIZATIONAL MEETING   *Salida Mail*, April 10, 1917.

VOTING IN BEN DISMAN   "Ben Disman Heads Red Cross; Strong
Organization Formed," *Salida Mail*, April 13, 1917. Ben was the owner
of Ben Disman's Clothing Co. in the Central Block at First & F Streets.

RED CROSS HOSPITAL   *Salida Mail*, April 13, 1917.

LATER THAT MONTH   "Be at Depot Sunday at 12:45; Salida Soldier
Boys Leave," *Salida Mail*, April 13, 1917.

"ALL SALIDA TURNED OUT"   "Immense Crowd Bids Goodbye to
Salida Recruits at Depot," *Salida Mail*, April 17, 1917.

THE UNITED STATES GOVERNMENT   *Salida Mail*, May 18, 1917. See
also: "The American Red Cross and Local Response to the 1918

Influenza Pandemic: A Four-City Case Study," by Marian Moser Jones. *Public Health Reports*, 2010 Supplement 3/Volume 125.

"NIMBLE FINGERS ARE BUSY"   "Red Cross Work Speeds Up with Much Help Needed," *Salida Mail*, July 13, 1917.

"THE YARN WILL BE SUPPLIED"   "Salida Red Cross Makes Big Record in Sewing for Army; To Hold Knitting Classes," *Salida Mail*, October 26, 1917.

JAMES RAMEY   "Ramey's New Song Published; First Edition Arrives," *Salida Mail*, June 1, 1917.

WHAT IS MOST CERTAIN   Michaela E. Nickol and Jason Kindrachuk, "A Year of Terror and a Century of Reflection: Perspectives o the Great Influenza Pandemic of 1918-1919," *BMC Infectious Diseases*, (2019) 19:117.

ON OCTOBER 15th   "Salida Has 200 Influenza Cases; Death Takes Two in One Family," *Salida Mail*, October 15, 1918.

THREE DAYS LATER   "Epidemic Holds City in Grip; Seven Deaths Reported to Date; Denton Hotel Made Hospital," *Salida Mail*, October 18, 1918.

73 PATIENTS FILLED   "One Death Today; 30 New Cases: Flu Has Not Reached Its Crest; Eighteen Deaths Since Outbreak," *Salida Mail*, October 22, 1918.

"WHOLE FAMILIES ARE DOWN"   "Epidemic Holds City in Grip; Seven Deaths Reported to Date; Denton Hotel Made Hospital," *Salida Mail*, October 18, 1918.

EIGHTEEN PEOPLE WERE   "One Death Today; 30 New Cases: Flu Has Not Reached Its Crest; Eighteen Deaths Since Outbreak," *Salida Mail*, October 22, 1918.

PNEUMONIA JACKETS   "Epidemic Holds City in Grip; Seven Deaths Reported to Date; Denton Hotel Made Hospital," *Salida Mail*, October 18, 1918.

"INFLUENZA IS FASTENING"   Ibid.

FATHER GALLAGHER   Ibid.

DENVER HAD REPORTEDLY "One Death Today; 30 New Cases: Flu Has Not Reached Its Crest; Eighteen Deaths Since Outbreak," *Salida Mail*, October 22, 1918.

GUNNISON WAS ONE OF Stephen J. Leonard, "The 1918 Influenza Outbreak: An Unforgettable Legacy," *Colorado Magazine*, No. 9, 1989.

INFLUENZA COMMITTEE "One Death Today; 30 New Cases: Flu Has Not Reached Its Crest; Eighteen Deaths Since Outbreak," *Salida Mail*, October 22, 1918.

LOCAL MADAM LAURA EVANS George Koenig, Interview by Gwen Perschbacher, November 8, 2003, transcript, Salida Regional Library Oral History Collection, Salida Regional Library, Salida, Colorado, http://salidaarchive.info/wp-content/uploads/2014/12/George-Koenig.pdf

FOOD WAS GATHERED "Influenza Notice," *Salida Mail*, October 22, 1918.

"THESE NURSES ARE WEARING OUT" "One Death Today; 30 New Cases: Flu Has Not Reached Its Crest; Eighteen Deaths Since Outbreak," *Salida Mail*, October 22, 1918.

DOGS AND CATS WERE CARRIERS "Dogs and Cats to be Destroyed Unless Confined Inside Yards; Flu Germs Carried By Animals," *Salida Mail*, Novermber 1, 1918.

1918 PANDEMIC STRUCK Michaela E. Nickol and Jason Kindrachuk, "A Year of Terror and a Century of Reflection: Perspectives on the Great Influenza Pandemic of 1918-1919," *BMC Infectious Diseases*, (2019) 19:117.

HERD IMMUNITY the state of a large proportion of the population to repel infectious disease. Vaccination is one way to effectively treat a large group against disease. This protects more susceptible members of the group who will then be less likely to contract disease.

ABOUT TWO BILLION PEOPLE The numbers in this paragraph are rough estimates: 2 billion is an approximate from the United Nations Department of Economic and Social Affairs. Nickol and Kindrachuk's paper is the source for infections and deaths worldwide from the pandemic. Arlene Shovald's series on the

"Epidemic of 1918" is the source for Salida's death count, *Mountain Mail*, October 28, 1993. Another interesting source for statistical information is the Department of Commerce Bureau of Census report, Mortality Statistics 1920, published 1922.

QUARANTINE WAS PARTIALLY LIFTED   "No New Cases of Flu Reported; Quarantine to be Lifted Monday," *Salida Mail*, December 31, 1918.

QUARANTINE WAS COMPLETELY LIFTED   "Quarantine is to be Lifted Next Monday," *Salida Record*, March 7, 1919.

"[LAURA] LOVED THE RED CROSS"   "Obituary," *Salida Mail*, December 31, 1918.

Thirty - The Beginning of a Tradition

AN EXPLOSIVE SHELL KILLED   "Military Funeral Sunday Will Honor Corporal Ray Lines," *Salida Mail*, April 21, 1922.

OVER 2,500 U.S. SOLDIERS   Patrick McSherry, "Casualties During the Spanish American War," http://www.spanamwar.com/casualties.htm

OVER 100,000 DIED   Carol R. Byerly, "War Losses (USA)," October 8, 2014, https://encyclopedia.1914-1918-online.net/article/war_losses_usa

POSSIBLY 70,000   Drew Lindsay, "Rest in Peace? Bringing Home U.S. War Dead," September 2012, historynet.com

SALIDA HELD A MILITARY   "Military Honors for War Hero; All Salida Pays Homage to Funeral of Corporal Ray Lines," *Salida Mail*, April 25, 1922.

Thirty-One - Salida's First Flight

"THE FIRST PLANE TO TAKE"   "Aeroplane Week at Salida, August 11-17," *Chaffee County Democrat*, August 9, 1919. "Crewdson To Give Free Flight; City to Furnish New Plane; Reception at Elks Club Planned," *Salida Mail*, July 8, 1919.

THE FIRST AEROPLANE FLIGHT   "Salida and State on Tiptoe
Waiting for Two-Day Fiesta; Biggest Crowd on Record Coming,"
Salida Mail, July 1, 1919.

MOST PEOPLE IN CHAFFEE   "Two-Day Fourth of July Program Will
Draw From Half of State," *Salida Mail*, June 6, 1919.

"ILLUMINATED FLIGHT WITH FIREWORKS"   *Chaffee County
Democrat*, May 31, 1919.

"WE HAVE NO OBJECTION"   "Girls Insist on Aeroplaning," *Salida
Mail*, June 10, 1919.

"WHAT! HARRY B. CREWDSON!"   "Army Flying Man Discovers
Salida Aviator is his Chum; Best in World; Says Visitor," *Salida Mail*,
June 20, 1919.

PONCHA BOULEVARD WOULD BE   "Salida and State on Tiptoe
Waiting for Two Day Fiesta; Biggest Crowd on Record Coming,"
Salida Mail, July 1, 1919.

FOR FIFTY CENTS ADMISSION   "Salida is Ready for Crowd;
Crewdson Arrives with Plane; Stables Filled with Horses," *Salida
Mail*, July 4, 1919.

"LOOPING THE LOOP"   "Crewdson, Dean of Airmen Tells How It
Happened," *Salida Mail*, July 8, 1919.

HARRY'S PLANE THAT DAY   "Crewdson Adjusts Aeroplane Engine
to this Altitude," *Salida Mail*, August 15, 1919.

"HE VOLPLANED WITHIN"   "Crewdson Falls with Aeroplane; City
Entertains Biggest Crowd That Ever Gathered in Salida," *Salida Mail*,
July 8, 1919.

HARRY ONLY SUFFERED   "Crewdson, Dean of Airmen, Tells How It
Happened," *Salida Mail*, July 8, 1919.

"IN THE HIGHER ALTITUDES"   "Crewdson Adjusts Aeroplane
Engine To This Altitude," *Salida Mail*, August 15, 1919.

"IT IS TOO BAD"   "Crewdson Falls with Aeroplane; City Entertains
Biggest Crowd That Ever Gathered in Salida," *Salida Mail*, July 8,
1919.

THE TOWN TOOK SUBSCRIPTIONS   "Committee to Get
Subscriptions for Salida Aeroplane This Week," *Salida Mail*, July 15,
1919.
IT WAS GUARANTEED TO   "Crewdson's Plane to Be Sent From New
York on August 6," *Salida Mail*, August 1, 1919.
AEROPLANE, CHRISTENED 'SALIDA'   "U.S. Navy Band to Play Here
and Crewdson to Fly Monday; Entire Program Free to Public," *Salida
Mail*, August 8, 1919.
GREAT CROWD OF HUNDREDS   "Crewdson to Fly This Evening;
Plane is Admired by Callers," *Salida Mail*, August 12, 1919.
"SPECIALLY CONSTRUCTED HIGH PRESSURE"   "Crewdson's Plane
to Be Sent from New York on August 6," *Salida Mail*, August 1, 1919.
"THE DESIGNERS AND AVIATORS"   "Crewdson Adjust Aeroplane
Engine to this Altitude," *Salida Mail*, August 15, 1919.
THE AIRPLANE, 'SALIDA'   "Hope of Aeroplane Flight is
Abandoned," *Salida Mail*, August 19, 1919.

Thirty-Two - Burning Crosses on Tenderfoot

THEIR BIGGEST PRESENCE WAS   Linda Gordon, *The Second Coming
of the KKK* (New York: Liveright Publishing Corporation, a division
of W.W. Norton & Company, 2018).
"AFTER ITS ESTABLISHMENT"   James H. Davis, "Colorado Under
the Klan," *Colorado Magazine*, vol. 42, no. 2 (Denver, Colo.: State
Historical Society of Colorado, 1965), 93-108.
"WE ARE PROUD"   "Klan Presents Salida Pastor with Substantial
Gift," *Chaffee County Republican*, January 25, 1924.
THE KKK BURNED   "Cross on Tenderfoot is Lighted by Cranks,"
Salida Mail, January 8, 1924.
A CROSS WAS BURNED   "A Fiery Cross Burned Brightly Tuesday
Night," *Chaffee County Republican*, April 4, 1924.
A PICNIC WAS HELD   "Klans Hold Picnic," *Chaffee County
Republican*, June 12, 1924.

"ALL DRESSED IN THE"   "Ku Klux Klan Have Organized in Buena Vista," *Chaffee County Republican*, June 13, 1924.

THE LOCAL PAPERS HAD   "200 Klansmen in Parade Sunday," *Salida Record*, June 13, 1924.

"AS THEY STARTED"   "Parade in Salida was Thrilling," *Chaffee County Republican*, June 13, 1924.

"THERE WAS A KU KLUX KLAN"   Stan Provenza, interview by Beth Smith, June 1, 2004, transcript, Salida Regional Library Oral History Collection, Salida Regional Library, Salida, Colorado, http://salidaarchive.info/wp-content/uploads/2014/12/Provenza.pdf

"THE SEIZURE OF MUNICIPALITIES"   James H. Davis, "Colorado Under the Klan," *Colorado Magazine*, vol. 42, no. 2 (Denver, Colo.: State Historical Society of Colorado, 1965), 93-108.

BY 1925 A MAJORITY   "Governor Does Not Ask Any Advice of Central Committee," *Salida Daily Record*, January 24, 1925.

KLAN OBJECTIVES   James H. Davis, "Colorado Under the Klan," *Colorado Magazine*, vol. 42, no. 2 (Denver, Colo.: State Historical Society of Colorado, 1965), 93-108.

A TOTAL OF SIX   Ibid. See also: "Klan Issue Coming to Head in State Capitol," *Salida Daily Record*, February 3, 1925.

ONE OF FRANK'S FELLOW   Ibid.

THE REPUBLICAN/DEMOCRATIC COALITION   Ibid.

"THE PEOPLE OF COLORADO"   Ibid.

Thirty-Three - The Making of Spiral Drive

COMMERCIAL CLUB   i.e. a group of businessmen dedicated to the economic benefits of the city.

FOR THE NEXT FEW MONTHS   "Volunteers Throw Bulwarks, Also Picks, on Mt. Tenderfoot," *Salida Mail*, February 14, 1922.

"CLOSE CORPORATION"   Ibid.

"COME OUT WITH A PICK"   Ibid.

"WASHINGTON'S BIRTHDAY"   "Proclamation," *Salida Mail*, February 21, 1922.

ABOUT 150 PEOPLE   "Business Men Turn Out to Work on
Tenderfoot Road," *Salida Mail*, February 24, 1922.
"CUT LONG STRETCHES"   "Railroad Men Make Big Gain on
Tenderfoot Road Project," *Salida Mail*, March 24, 1922.
"FULL OF PEP"   "Song About Tenderfoot Road," *Salida Mail*, March
31, 1922.
HAMPSON WAS THE CHAIRMAN   "Warden Capp on Road Again;
Ladies Auxiliaries to Give Cooking Sales for Road Fund," *Salida Mail*,
April 4, 1922.
A GENTLE RIVALRY   "$100 Cleared By Auxiliaries for Tenderfoot
Road Fund," *Salida Mail*, April 11, 1922 & "Tenderfoot Thursday to Be
Regular Event," *Salida Mail*, March 7, 1922.
AND TO RAISE FUNDS   "Home Cooking Sale Saturday; Another
Boost for Road Fund," *Salida Mail*, April 18, 1922.
"GIVE ME ONE DAY"   "Warden Capp Will Build Road Up
Tenderfoot Mountain in Day," *Salida Mail*, March 14, 1922.
DENVER & RIO GRANDE RAILROAD DONATED   "Reformatory Boys,
150 Strong, Coming in Special Train to Work on Tenderfoot Road,"
Salida Mail, March 28, 1922.
AT THE END OF MARCH   "Road Difficulties Melt When Warden
Capp Tackles the Job," *Salida Mail*, March 31, 1922.
"EVERY STRAY ELK"   "Elks Horn In on Tenderfoot For Big Day Next
Thursday," *Salida Mail*, April 18, 1922.
"NEARLY 200 MEN"   "Elks Day on Tenderfoot Road Draws Big
Crowd of Workers," *Salida Mail*, April 21, 1922.
THEN ON JULY 1st   "Shopmen Answer Strike Call; All But One Quit
Work Here," *Salida Mail*, July 4, 1922.
BY MID-JULY   "Big Day on Tenderfoot; Strikers Work on Road,"
Salida Mail, July 14, 1922.
SALIDA CHAMBER OF COMMERCE   "Salida Greets Pueblo Boosters
Who Are Making Tour of State," *Salida Mail*, September 12, 1922.
"SALIDA PRESENTS AN UNUSUAL"   "Salida, Live One, Says
Peterson of Colorado U," *Salida Mail*, October 6, 1922.

Thirty-Four - The 1929 Air Circus

TEN YEARS AFTER   see Salida's First Flight, chapter thirty.

SEND MAIL BY AIRPLANE   "Air Mail Officer Visits Salida; Urges Building of Airport Here," *Salida Mail*, May 7, 1929.

"THIS NEW DIRECT AIRMAIL"   Nolie Mumey, *Epitome of the Semi-Centennial History of Colorado's Airmail* (Denver, Colorado: The Range Press, 1977).

THE LEGION BOUGHT   "Legion Purchases Land for Airport: Aerial Circus Planned for Two Days," *Salida Mail*, June 7, 1929.

"THE FIELD PURCHASED BY"   "American Legion Secures Airport to Place Salida on Airways," *Salida Record*, June 7, 1929.

"LANDED THREE POINTS"   "First Plane Makes Perfect Landing on Highest Field in the World," *Salida Mail*, June 25, 1929. Thomas Nevens accompanied Red on his historic flight and became the first Salidan to fly out of the new American Legion Airport.

AN AIR CIRCUS WAS   "Salida Legion Airport," *Salida Record*, June 14, 1929.

THE ONLY COST WAS   "Airplane Mail Urged to Advertise Salida," *Salida Mail*, July 3, 1929.

"UNDER THE AUSPICES OF"   "July 3, 4 Dedication of the new Salida Legion Airport [advertisement]," *Salida Mail*, June 18, 1929. "Salida's Air Circus July 3 and 4 Attracting State Wide Attention." *Salida Mail*, June 18, 1929.

THE Y&R AUTO COMPANY   "Y. & R. Auto Co. Purchases First Airplane Owned in Salida," *Salida Mail*, June 28, 1929.

BOTTLE OF WATER MELTED   "First Plane Makes Perfect Landing on Highest Field in the World," *Salida Mail*, June 25, 1929.

DAREDEVIL JIMMY DONOHUE   "Salida's Air Circus July 3 and 4 Attracting State Wide Attention," *Salida Mail*, June 18, 1929.

"HE MADE THREE PARACHUTE"   "Two-Day Celebration is Big Success; Crowds Thrilled by Daring Air Stunts," *Salida Mail*, July 5, 1929.

"LT. O'CONNOR THRILLED"   Ibid.

"OFFICIALS AND CITIZENS"   "Air Mail Bulletin Comments on
Salida Airport and Future Air Route," *Salida Record*, July 30, 1929.
"PILOT CARR, THE FLYING FOOL"   "Interest in Flying School Here is
Increasing," *Salida Record*, August 2, 1929.
CARCO AIR SERVICE   "Carco Airlines," Cavalcade of Wings,
www.albcow.com/carco_airlines.html

Thirty-Five - The Hermit of Arbor Villa

YOUNG FRANK GIMLETT   "Life Ended Friday Night for Hermit of
Arbor Villa," *Salida Daily-Mail Record*, February 4, 1952.
FAMOUS COLUMBUS MINE   "Gimlet's Maverick Mine," *Salida Mail*,
November 23, 1909.
SALIDA WOOD & LUMBER   "Salida Wood and Lumber Supply
Company," *Salida Mail*, July 4, 1905.
HIS BUSINESS WAS SUCCESSFUL   *Salida Mail*, September 13, 1910.
ALSO BUILT 129 & 139   "Work Commenced on New Theater," *Salida
Mail*, July 7, 1911. See also a small item under "Municipal Authorities
Muzzle Saloon Business," *Salida Record*, July 7, 1911 and "Ideal Auto
Company are in New Quarters," *Salida Mail*, December 19, 1913.
PURCHASED THE SALIDA OPERA   "Local News Notes," *Salida Mail*,
July 18, 1911. The September 12, 1911 issue of the Salida Mail
included the following: "F.E. Gimlett has had painted a huge sign for
the opera house. This sign runs down the full length of the front of
the building and the words 'Empress Theater' appear thereon. A
number of electric lights from the side show up the sign in fine
shape."
AFTERMATH OF A FIRE   "Fire Destroys Gimlett Building; $50,000
Loss, Partly Insured," *Salida Mail*, July 17, 1925.
FRANK SOON ABANDONED   The Salida city directories of the 1940s
show in their listings a Mrs. F.E. Gimlett, minus her husband.
"TODAY I SIT ALONE"   F.E. Gimlett, *Over Trails of Yesterday*, book one
(1943), 7.

HERMIT OFTEN MADE TRIPS   "Old Colorado Miner Creates Sensation in Washington," *Steamboat Pilot*, November 11, 1943.
"GREAT ALARM"   F.E. Gimlett, *Over Trails of Yesterday*, book seven (1948) 61.
"DEFLATE GOLD TO ITS OLD"   F.E. Gimlett, *Over Trails of Yesterday*, book seven (1948) 62.
DRESS UP AS SANTA   Orville Wright [letter to the editor], "Christmas in Salida," *Colorado Central*, January 1, 2008, https://coloradocentralmagazine.com/christmas-in-salida/
SALIDA'S MOST MEMORABLE CHARACTERS   In the August 11, 1941 edition of the Salida Daily Mail, it was reported that "Frank E. Gimlett, the Hermit of Arbor Villa, is holding forth near Third and F Street with a prospector camp. He has a tent equipped with a pine bough bed. A campfire burns in front of the camp and the burro, tied to the fence, sings his canary notes every few minutes. The hermit has a crowd of visitors around him most of the time."
"NOW I HAVE REACHED"   F.E. Gimlett, *Over Trails of Yesterday*, book seven (1948) 16.

Thirty-Six - Leonidas and His Spartans

TYPICALLY OUTWEIGHED SALIDA   "Spartans Open Season Saturday; Meet South Denver High Here," *Salida Mail*, September 18, 1934.
FOR THE FIRST TIME   "Spartans Lose to Trinidad and Flu; Salida Team Closes Brilliant Season," *Salida Mail*, December 6, 1932.
"THE BEST KNOWN MAN"   "Coach White Hero of Salida Team Develops Two Sets of Champions," *Salida Mail*, November 14, 1933.
"NOTHING CAN STOP 'EM NOW"   "Salida Wins Classic; Special Train Overcrowded," *Salida Mail*, October 31, 1933.
MORE THAN 500 PEOPLE   "Salida Wallops Canon City Tigers; Spartans Practically Clinch Pennant," *Salida Mail*, October 31, 1933.
"SCUDDER, SPARK PLUG OF THE LINE"   "Spartans Leave Friday to Enter State Finals," *Salida Mail*, December 5, 1933.

"THE ENTIRE JUNIOR-SENIOR"   "Spartans Leave for Loveland
Game; High School Students See Them Off," *Salida Mail*, December 8,
1933.

THOSE WHO DIDN'T RIDE   "State Champions," *Salida Mail*,
December 12, 1933.

"WINDING UP A PERFECT"   "Spartans Win State Championship
Defeating Loveland Indians 26-7," *Salida Mail*, December 12, 1933.

"IF ONE LISTENED"   "State Champions," *Salida Mail*, December 12,
1933.

"IF THERE ARE ANY HALOS"   Ibid.

"THE HIGH SCHOOL WAS IN"   Ibid.

"OLD KING FOOTBALL"   "Spartan Champs Facing Big Test: Nine
1933 Stars Are Out of Team," *Salida Mail*, September 14, 1934.

FERA   Federal Emergency Relief Administration

"EVERY CLASS FROM THE"   "SHS Homecoming Parade Saturday
Will Precede Pueblo Central Game," *Salida Mail*, October 19, 1934.

"IT GOES WITHOUT SAYING"   "Spartans Beat Centennial 14 to 0;
Again South Central League Champs," *Salida Mail*, November 13,
1934.

"THE SPARTANS LIKELY WILL"   "Spartans Ready for Trinidad
Tussle; Team Will Leave Salida Wednesday," *Salida Mail*, November
27, 1934.

IN PREPARATION   "Salida Awaits Final Game Saturday; Tickets
Selling Fast for Contest," *Salida Mail*, December 7, 1934.

"THE BIGGEST CLASSIC SALIDA"   "Fort Collins Team Arrives Today
Ready for State Contest Saturday," *Salida Mail*, December 7, 1934.

"COACH WHITE WILL ATTEND"   Ibid.

"ATTEMPTED AN END AROUND"   "Spartans Made Safety in the
Last Period," *Salida Mail*, December 11, 1934.

"THE LAMBKINS WERE TOUGH"   "Visitors Give Hard Battle to
White Men," *Salida Mail*, December 11, 1934.

"THE SALIDA SPARTANS SERVED"   "Spartans Score 13th Conference
Win Saturday by Defeating Centennial 33-0," *Salida Mail*, October 8,
1935.

"THE SPARTANS 13-6 ADVANTAGE"   "Salida Football Fans Near Heart Failure At End of Close Game in Canon," *Salida Mail*, October 15, 1935.

"SALIDA WAS IN DANGER"   "Frankie Gentile Runs 60 Yards to Score in Few Closing Minutes," *Salida Mail*, December 6, 1935.

DENVER & RIO GRANDE BRAKEMAN   "J.S. Ritchie is Decorator of Special Train Engine," *Salida Mail*, December 17, 1935.

"ALL AGREED THAT THE SPARTANS"   "Grand Junction Falls Before White's Squad in Final State Contest," *Salida Mail*, December 17, 1935.

THAT YEAR, THREE SPARTANS   "Three Spartans Named for All State Team," *Salida Mail*, December 17, 1935.

Thirty-Seven - A Spartan Tragedy

"BEGINNING WITH A SCRUBBY"   "White Has Guided the Spartans Through 39 Straight Victories," *Salida Record*, November 27, 1936.

"BRENTON ENTERED"   "Oliver Brenton, Football Star, Killed," *Salida Daily Mail*, January 11, 1937.

"COACH WHITE WAS SO DISTRAUGHT"   Ibid.

"COACH WHITE AND BRENTON"   Ibid.

"BRENTON, GREATEST HIGH SCHOOL"   "Sports Writer Gives Eulogy of Brenton," *Salida Daily Mail*, January 11, 1937.

BUT THEN RESIGNED   "Coach Harold A. White to Leave Salida at Close of Term," *Salida Record*, May 25, 1937.

"HE RECEIVED AT LEAST"   "Former SHS Gridders Honor Coach," *Mountain Mail*, July 25, 1977.

"A SUPPLY OF BLANKETS"   "Coach White's Superstitions Disclosed by L.A.B.," *Salida Record*, October 9, 1936.

"BIG FLOYD (TUFFY) CHAMBERS"   "White Has Guided the Spartans Through 39 Straight Victories," *Salida Record*, November 27, 1936.

Thirty-Eight - Salida Ski Train

SALIDA SKI CLUB WAS FOUNDED   "Winter Sports Club Organized Last Night," *Salida Record*, September 17, 1937.

THE SKIERS COULD UNLOAD   "Finest Ski Course in Colo. is Report of Inspector," *Salida Daily Mail*, September 21, 1937.

DEEMED IT "PERFECT"   Ibid.

T.J. FLYNN WAS APPOINTED   "Moving Pictures and Lecture Friday Night at Isis Theatre," *Salida Record*, December 14, 1937.

"ABOARD THE NARROW GAUGE"   "Forty Enjoy Winter Sports on Marshall Pass Sunday," *Salida Record*, January 11, 1938.

FREE VISIT TO THE SALIDA HOT SPRINGS   "Ski Club Plans Special Marshall Pass Train Feb. 13," *Salida Record*, January 21, 1938.

"YOU DO NOT HAVE TO BE"   Ibid.

GUNNISON HEARD ABOUT   "Gunnison Also Plans to Run Marshall Pass Special Feb. 13," *Salida Record*, February 1, 1938.

A GROUP OF PUEBLOANS   "Pueblo to Send Special Train to Join Salida Ski Fans Feb. 13," *Salida Record*, February 1, 1938.

SOLD-OUT DENVER & RIO GRANDE   "Marshall Pass Ski Course and Hot Water Pool Formally Opened," *Salida Daily Mail*, February 14, 1938.

THE SKIERS DISEMBARKED   Ibid.

IT HAD BEEN DESIGNATED   "Finest Ski Course in Colo. Is Report of Inspector," *Salida Daily Mail*, September 21, 1937.

THE GUNNISON DELEGATION   "First Snow Train to Marshall Pass Is Tremendous Success," *Salida Record,* February 15, 1938.

COUNT PHILLIPE DE PRET   "Railroad Wires For Extra Coaches to Accommodate Ski Enthusiasts," *Salida Record*, February 11, 1938.

EXHIBITION SKI RACE   "First Snow Train to Marshall Pass Is Tremendous Success," *Salida Record,* February 15, 1938.

"THOSE WHO DID NOT"   "Marshall Pass Ski Course and Hot Water Pool Formally Opened," *Salida Daily Mail*, February 14, 1938.

CELEBRATED UNTIL 10 O'CLOCK   Ibid.

NEW, MODERN MONARCH PASS   "Modern Highway Completed Over Rockies on U.S. 50," *Salida Record*, November 21, 1939.
SALIDA SKI CLUB, THE U.S.F.S.   "Application Made For Winter Sports WPA Project at Monarch," and "Winter Sports Meeting Draws Large Crowd," *Salida Record*, January 19, 1940.
MONARCH SKI RESORT OPENED   "Winter Sports Area to Be Dedicated Sat. and Sun.," *Salida Record*, February 16, 1940.
ONLY RAN FOR TWO WINTERS   T. Rex Rhodes, interview by Beth Smith, April 4, 2006, transcript, Salida Regional Library Oral History Collection, Salida Regional Library, Salida, Colorado, http://salidaarchive.info/wp-content/uploads/2014/12/Rhodes.pdf
"AT THE [SALIDA] DEPOT"   Bob Biglow, interview by Beth Smith, March 12, 2005, transcript, Salida Regional Library Oral History Collection, Salida Regional Library, Salida, Colorado, http://salidaarchive.info/wp-content/uploads/2014/12/Bob-Biglow.pdf
THE MARSHALL PASS RAIL LINE   "Marshall Pass Main Line: D&RG / D&RGW Marshall Pass Route History," http://www.drgw.net/info/MarshallPass

Thirty-Nine - The Miracle of Television

PLANS FOR A COMMUNITY   "Texans Plan Application for Community TV Service," *Salida Daily Mail-Record*, May 11, 1954.
CITY COUNCIL AGREED   "City Council Picks Texans TV Proposal," *Salida Daily Mail-Record*, July 20, 1954.
"ODDLY ENOUGH, ON THE SITE"   "Television Truly Miracle," *Salida Daily-Mail Record*, October 28, 1954.
COMPANY HELD A DINNER   "Television Dealers Guests at Dinner," *Salida Daily Mail-Record*, October 8, 1954.
"I WOULD SAY THAT THE PICTURE"   "Committee Praises Picture Seen at TV Antenna Site," *Salida Daily Mail-Record*, October 12, 1954.
THE LOCAL PAPER PUBLISHED   "TV Comes to Salida," *Salida Daily Mail-Record*, October 28, 1954.

OVER 3,000 PEOPLE ATTENDED   "Crowd Enthusiastic at Television Show," *Salida Daily Mail-Record*, November 1, 1954.

"ALL SORTS AND KINDS"   Ibid.

"LOOK WHAT WE HAVE BEEN"   Ibid.

IT WAS $125   "City Council Picks Texans TV Proposal," *Salida Daily Mail-Record*, July 20, 1954.

ENTIRE TOWN HAD BEEN WIRED   "Extending TV To the West Side," *Salida Daily Mail-Record*, November 26, 1954.

200 HOMES HAD TV   "TV Company Finishes Wiring," *Salida Daily Mail-Record*, December 23, 1954.

SALIDANS STARTED WITH   Ibid.

SALIDA TV CABLE COMPANY RENAMED   "Television Company Headquartering Here," *Salida Daily Mail-Record*, February 2, 1955.

ANTENNA SYSTEM WAS INSTALLED   "Channel 4 Available Dec. 1 From New Antenna on Methodist," *Mountain Mail*, November 11, 1956.

Forty - Chaffee County Opus

THIS MASSIVE UNDERTAKING   June Shaputis, "The Clay Family Place Newsletter Biography Page," 2001, http://jshaputis.tripod.com/ClayBios/JuneShaputisBio.htm

"HENTSCHELL WAS ALONE"   "Prospector Found Dead," *Salida Mail*, September 30, 1910.

"FROM THE INFIRMITIES OF HER"   "Death of Mrs. Judith Gill," *Salida Mail*, July 2, 1901.

"THE HUSTLE AND BUSTLE"   "Death of John Jay, Sr., Thins Ranks of Chaffee County Pioneers," *Mountain Mail*, March 13, 1957.

"...IT WAS NAMED FOR ONE"   "George H. Pugh, Pioneer Coloradoan, Dies This Morning," *Salida Daily Mail*, June 3, 1938.

"IN MAY 1860, HERMAN"   "Judge Max Dickman Dead; Oldest Colorado Native," *Salida Daily Mail*, October 3, 1945.

"IN HONOR OF O'HAVER'S"   "Services Held Tuesday for T.R. O'Haver," *Mountain Mail*, September 18, 1969.

"HE TOOK UP THE TRACT"   "Thomas Cameron: The Oldest Settler in the Valley Has Been Called to His Final Rest and Reward," *Salida Mail*, August 31, 1897.

"DEATH CAME THIS MORNING"   "Picturesque Miner Often Rich, Poor, Called By Death," *Salida Daily Mail*, May 7, 1948.

"I BELIEVE, RICH OR POOR"   June Shaputis, "The Clay Family Place Newsletter Biography Page," 2001, http://jshaputis.tripod.com/ClayBios/JuneShaputisBio.htm

"HAUNTED LOCAL CEMETERIES"   "June Marie Shaputis obituary," *Mountain Mail*, October 28, 2019.

Bibliography

Books & Manuscripts

Baker, James H. & Hafen, Leroy R, *History of Colorado*. Denver: Linderman Co., Inc., 1927.

Baldwin, James, *The Fire Next Time*. New York: Vintage International, 1991.

Bancroft, Hubert Howe, "The Extermination of the Indians," *Works by Hubert Howe Bancroft, vol. 24*. San Francisco: The History Company, Publishers, 1887.

Bauer, William H., Ozment, James L., Willard, John H. *Colorado Post Offices, 1859-1989: A Comprehensive Listing of Post Offices, Stations, and Branches*. Golden, Colo.: The Colorado Railroad Museum, 1990.

Bernardi, Gayle K. and Thomas W. Segady, Thomas W., "The Development of African American Newspapers in the American

West," *African Americans on the Western Frontier.* Boulder, Colorado: University Press of Colorado, 2001.

Brigham, Lillian (Rice), *Historical Guide to Colorado: A Pilgrimage Over the Old Trails to Outstanding Sites and Landmarks.* Denver, Colo.: The W.H. Kistler Stationery Co., 1931.

Carver, Jack, et al., *Colorado: Land of Legend.* Denver: Caravon Press, 1959.

Chapman, Arthur, *The Story of Colorado: Out Where the West Begins.* Chicago: Rand McNally & Company, 1924.

Chappell, Gordon, *Scenic Line of the World.* Originally published in Colorado Rail Annual 1970. Golden, Colo.: Colorado Railroad Museum, [1970].

Collman, Russ, ed. *Trails Among the Columbine. 1991/1992. Salida, Colorado, Denver & Rio Grande Railroad Town: A Colorado High Country Anthology.* Denver: Sundance Publications Limited, 1992.

Collman, Russ, ed. *Trails Among the Columbine. 1993/1994. The Monarch Branch of the Denver & Rio Grande Railway: A Colorado High County Anthology.* Denver: Sundance Publications Limited, 1994.

Crawford, R.D., *Geology and Ore Deposits of the Monarch and Tomichi Districts, Colorado.* Bulletins 4 and 5. Denver, Colo.: Smith-Brooks Printing Co., 1913.

Davis, Clyde Brion, *The Arkansas.* New York: Farrar & Rinehart, Inc., 1940.

Dorchester, Daniel, *The Liquor Problem in All Ages.* New York: Phillips & Hunt, 1884.

Dougherty, Samuel A., *Railroad Tall Tales (And Other B.S.)* Grand Junction, CO: Printmasters, 1992.

Emerson, E.R., "History of Chaffee County," *History of the Arkansas Valley, Colorado.* Chicago: O.L. Baskin & Co., 1881.

Ensign, Edgar T., "A Plea for Rocky Mountain Forests." Proceedings of the American Forestry Congress at Its Meeting Held at Atlanta, Ga., December, 1888. Washington: Gibson Bros., Printers and Bookbinders, 1889.

Everett, George and Hutchinson, Wendell, *Under the Angel of Shavano*. Denver, Colorado: Golden Bell Press, 1963.

Fossett, Frank, *Colorado: Its Gold and Silver Mines, Farms and Stock Ranges, and Health and Pleasure Resorts. Tourist's Guide to the Rocky Mountains.* Second Edition. New York: C.G Crawford, 1880.

Front Range Research Associates, Inc., *Downtown Salida Historic Buildings Survey, 2001-02: Final Report.* Denver, Colo., June 2003.

Front Range Research Associates, Inc., *Salida, Colorado Historic Buildings Survey, 2005-06: Final Survey Report.* Denver, Colo.

F.E. Gimlett, F.E., *Over Trails of Yesterday*, volumes 1-9. Salida, Colo.: Hermit of Arbor Villa, [dates vary].

Gordon, Linda, *The Second Coming of the KKK.* New York: Liveright Publishing Corporation, a division of W.W. Norton & Company, 2018.

Hall, Frank, *Colorado's Mineral Wealth.* Denver, Colo.: Colorado & Southern Railway, 1909.

Ham, David J., "Salida, Colorado, 1880-1886: The Transition From End-of-Track Construction Camp to Established Community." *Essays and Monographs in Colorado History*, 1983—Number 1, Colorado Historical Society.

Harper, Jane C., Leavitt, Craig W., Noel, Thomas J. *Colorado Newspapers: A History & Inventory, 1859-2000.* Denver: Colorado Press Association Foundation and Center for Colorado & the West at Auraria Library, 2014.

Helmers, Dow, *Historic Alpine Tunnel.* Denver: Sage Books, 1963.

Henderson, Charles, *Mining in Colorado: A History of Discovery, Development, and Production.* Professional Paper 138. Washington, D.C.: Government Printing Office, 1926.

Hill, James, *The Mining Districts of the Western United States.* USGS Bulletin. Washington, D.C., Government Printing Office, 1912.

Hollister, Ovando J., *The Mines of Colorado.* Springfield, Mass.: Samuel Bowles & Company, 1867.

Humbeutel, Lacy, "The Monte Cristo Hotel: Salida's Famous Railroad Stop." *Humbeutel Diaries*, Salida Regional Library, Salida, Colorado.

Ingersoll, Ernest, *The Crest of the Continent: A Summer's Ramble in the Rocky Mountains and Beyond.* Chicago: R.R. Donnelley & Sons, Publishers, 1885.

Jacobson, Mark I., *Antero Aquamarines.* Coeur D'Alene, ID: L.R. Ream Publishing, 1993.

Jefferson, James, Delaney, Robert W., and Thompson, Gregory C., *The Southern Utes: A Tribal History.* Ignacio, Colo.: Southern Ute Tribe, 1973.

Lee, Harry A., *Colorado: Report of the State Bureau of Mines, for the years 1901-2.* Denver, Colo.: The Smith-Brooks Printing Company, 1903.

LeMassena, Robert A., *Colorado's Mountain Railroads: Revised Edition.* Denver: Sundance Books, 1984.

MacKell, Jan, *Brothels, Bordellos, & Bad Girls: Prostitution in Colorado 1860-1930.* Albuquerque, N.M.: University of New Mexico Press, 2004.

Madley, Benjamin, *An American Genocide: The United States and the California Indian Catastrophe, 1846-1873.* New Haven ; London: Yale University Press, 2017.

Mitchell, Lori, et al., *Purple and White: Community, Glory, Tragedy.*

Mumey, Nolie, *Epitome of the Semi-Centennial History of Colorado's Airmail*. Denver, Colorado: The Range Press, 1977.

Murray, Charles A., et al., *Newspaper Career of E.D. Cowen with Biographic Sketches*. Seattle: Western Printing Company, 1930.

[Nims, F.C.] *Health, Wealth, and Pleasure in Colorado and New Mexico: A Reliable Treatise on the Famous Pleasure and Health Resorts, and the Rich Mining and Agricultural Regions of the Rocky Mountains.* Chicago: Belford, Clarke and Co., Publishers, 1881.

Rist, Martin, ed., *Brand Book 1969: Silver Anniversary Edition, Vol. 25.* Denver: The Westerners, 1970.

Sabin, Edwin L. *"Around the Circle": A Thousand Miles Through the Rockies, "Every Mile a Picture".* Colorado Springs, Colo.: Century One Press, [ca. 1976].

Smiley, Jerome C., *History of Denver*. Denver: Old Americana, 1978.

Thode, Jackson C., "A Century of Passenger Trains," *The 1970 Denver Westerners Brand Book*, (Boulder, Colo.: Johnson Publishing Company, 1972).

Toulmin, Priestley and Hammarstrom, Jane M. *Geology of the Mount Aetna Volcanic Center, Chaffee and Gunnison Counties, Colorado.* U.S. Geological Survey Bulletin 1864. United States Government Printing Office, 1990.

United States Department of Agriculture: Forest Service, "Vacation Trips in the Cochetopa National Forest" (1919).

United States Environmental Protection Agency. Region 8 (Denver, Colorado), *Smeltertown Superfund Site: Third Five Year Review, Chaffee County, Salida, CO*. Denver CO: U.S. EPA, 2015.

Warman, Cy, *Mountain Melodies*. Denver, Colo.: Cy Warman, 1892.

Warman, Cy, *The Prospector: Story of the Life of Nicholas C. Creede*. Denver: Great Divide Publishing Co., 1894.

Warman, Cy, *Short Rails*. New York: Charles Scribner's Sons, 1900.

Warman, Cy, *Songs of Cy Warman*. Boston: Rand Avery Co., 1911.

Wolle, Muriel Sibell, *Stampede to Timberline: The Ghost Towns and Mining Camps of Colorado*. Chicago: Sage Books, 1949.

X, Malcolm & Haley, Alex, *The Autobiography of Malcolm X*. New York: Grove Press, 1965.

Newspapers

The Colorado Historic Newspapers Database at the Colorado State Library, was the core resource for this book. Though most of the writing was inspired by some item from the Salida Archive, the database was usually the first place that I looked for any information relating to it.

The Salida Library's first foray into purchasing digitization occurred in 2015 when the library won a $6,500 SIPA grant. This was augmented with money from the Tuesday Evening Club, who gifted their remaining funds to the library. It was their parting gift to the library and the Club disbanded soon after.

Articles

Blakemore, Erin, "Five Things to Know About Pullman Porters," *Smithsonian*, June 30, 2016, https://www.smithsonianmag.com/smart-news/five-things-know-about-pullman-porters-180959663/.

Carroll, Richard, "The Founding of Salida," *Colorado Magazine*, vol. XI, no. 4, (July 1934) 121-133.

Davis, James H., "Colorado Under the Klan," *Colorado Magazine*, vol. 42, no. 2, (Spring 1965) 93-108.

Haase, Carl L., "Gothic, Colorado: City of Silver Wires," *Colorado Magazine*, vol. 51, no. 4, (Fall 1974) 294-316.

C.E. Hagie, C.E., "Gunnison in Early Days," *Colorado Magazine*, vol. 8, no. 4, (July 1931) 121-129.

Leonard, Stephen J., "The 1918 Influenza Outbreak: An Unforgettable Legacy," *Colorado Magazine*, No. 9, 1989.

Moore, Wallace, and Borland, Lois, "Quarrying the Granite for the State Capitol," *Colorado Magazine*, vol. XXIV, no. 2, (March 1947) 49-58.

Moser Jones, Marian, "The American Red Cross and Local Response to the 1918 Influenza Pandemic: A Four-City Case Study." *Public Health Reports*, 2010 Supplement 3/Volume 125.

Mumey, Nolie, "The 'Hogmaster' Poet of the Rockies," *Denver Westerners Monthly Roundup*, vol. 17, issue 5.

Nickol, Michaela E., and Kindrachuk, Jason, "A Year of Terror and a Century of Reflection: Perspectives o the Great Influenza Pandemic of 1918-1919," *BMC Infectious Diseases*, (2019) 19:117.

Stearly, Michael, "Archaeological Heritage of Colorado's Ute Tribe: Part of National Forests' History in Rocky Mountain Region," (U.S. Forest Service, 2015) https://www.fs.usda.gov/features/archaeological-heritage-colorados-ute-tribe-part-national-forests-history-rocky-mountain.

Williams, Jasmin K., "The Brotherhood of Sleeping Car Porters: The First Black Labor Union," *The New York Amsterdam News*, May 30-June 5, 2013.

Online Resources

Salida Historic Building Surveys. Front Range Research Associates were commissioned by the City of Salida to provide a detailed survey of the historic buildings in Salida. These were intensive surveys that recorded and evaluated properties within and adjacent to the historic commercial district. The project also conducted a reconnaissance level survey of the remainder of the city. All three of the surveys were funded by grants from the Colorado State Historical Fund with support from the City of Salida. These Colorado Cultural Resource Survey Forms are highly detailed records for many of the historic properties in Salida.

Sanborn Fire insurance Maps. Around 1850, American insurance companies felt the need to map out potential fire risks in communities around the country in order to determine insurance rates. The Sanborn Fire Insurance Company mapped out around 12,000 cities and towns in America, and Salida was one of these. These are the earliest maps of Salida and show a footprint of what buildings were where, the size and shape, and the type of business in occupancy. Occasionally, the name of the business will appear. The earliest maps of Salida date from 1883 and run through to 1914. They are housed at the University of Colorado, Boulder's website: https://cudl.colorado.edu/luna/servlet/view/all/where/Salida?sort=city%2Cdate%2Csheet
and at the Library of Congress:
https://www.loc.gov/collections/sanborn-maps/articles-and-essays/introduction-to-the-collection/

The Richard Carroll Collection & the Founding of Salida. The
Richard Carroll Collection is one part of History Colorado's CWA
Pioneer Interviews. This was a project where the State Historical
Society of Colorado (now History Colorado) received Civil Work
Administration funds in the 1930s and paid people to travel around
the state and gather stories from immigrants who were then still
living. Richard Eaton Carroll (1901-1987) was the interviewer for
Chaffee County. Richard Carroll also wrote a short history of Salida,
"The Founding of Salida" which was published in Colorado
magazine.
http://salidaarchive.info/richard-carroll-collection/

Chaffee County, Colorado, Burial Records - compiled by June
Shaputis.
http://usgwarchives.net/co/chaffee.htm

Salida City Directory Collection at the Salida Regional Library.
http://salidaarchive.info/archived-phone-books-and-city-directories/

Salida Regional Library Interviews:
http://salidaarchive.info/oral-histories/

The Thomas Nevens Papers, part of the Donna Nevens Collection.
http://salidaarchive.info/thomas-a-nevens-papers/

Tuesday Evening Club Papers, a selection of articles and essays
regarding the Salida Library's founding.
http://salidaarchive.info/tuesday-evening-club/

History of the Arkansas Valley, Colorado. Chicago : O.L. Baskin & Co., 1881.
https://babel.hathitrust.org/cgi/pt?id=wu.89064446123&view=1up&seq=87

History of the Cochetopa National Forest by Joseph M. Cuenin and Fred B. Agee, 1924.
http://salidaarchive.info/wp-content/uploads/2014/12/fred-agee.pdf

Image List and Credits

- Cover image: *Rocky Mountain Views on the Rio Grande, "The Scenic Line of the World": consisting of Twenty-Three Colored Views from Recent Photographs. Made exclusively for the Van Noy Inter-State Company, Denver, Colorado. For sale only en route on the Denver & Rio Grande Western Railroad.* Engraved, printed, and published by the Smith-Brooks Printing Company, Denver, Colorado, U.S.A. Copyright 1917 by Smith-Brooks Co.
- Frontispiece: *A Bird's Eye View of Salida.* Dick Dixon Collection, part of the larger Salida Centennial Photo Archive, Salida Regional Library.
- Epigraph: *A Bird's Eye View of Salida, ca. 1890.* Salida Museum Negatives Collection, Salida Regional Library.

2 *A Winter View of Salida.* Salida Museum Negatives Collection., Salida Regional Library.

10 *Current map of Ute Reservations in Utah and Colorado.* Used with permission of Southern Ute Indian Tribe.

15 *Map of Hidden Treasure of the Spaniards*, Salida Record, May 29, 1937.

17 *Denver & Rio Grande Engine No. 168.* Ca. 1900. Salida Centennial Collection, Salida Regional Library.

19 *Denver & Rio Grande Engine No. 106.* Bob Rush Collection, Salida Regional Library.

20 Meigs, Newell. *Denver & Rio Grande Roundhouse Turntable.* Ca. 1900. Virgil Jackson Collection, Salida Regional Library.

25 *Bateman Hardware Store at 119 F Street.* Ca. 1916. The Bateman Family Collection, Salida Regional Library.

26 *George Bateman.* The Bateman Family Collection, Salida Regional Library.

27 *Interior of Bateman Hardware Store.* Ca. 1895. The Bateman Family Collection, Salida Regional Library.

35 *Salida Hose Company No. 1.* 1883. Salida Fire Department, Salida Centennial Photo Collection, Salida Regional Library.

41 *Fire Company at 124 E Street.* Ca. 1903. Salida Fire Department, Salida Centennial Photo Collection, Salida Regional Library.

43 *Peter Mulvany. Groceries, Feed, Grain & Hay.* Donna Nevens Collection, Salida Regional Library.

44 *Peter Mulvany's First Street Empire.* History Colorado.

47 *The State Capital Map.* Mountain Mail, September 10, 1881.

53 *Baxter's Watch.* Author's photograph.

63 *Stingley Crime Scene.* Donna Nevens Collection, Salida Regional Library.

71 *Railroad Ties.* Image part of a powerpoint presentation by CSU Professor Mike Eckhoff.

73 *Trees on Tenderfoot Mountain.* March 20, 1895. Salida Centennial Collection, Salida Regional Library.

75 *Yard & Jester's Blacksmiths & Wagon Shop.* Ca. 1890. Patricia Bradbury Holton Collection, Salida Regional Library.

76 *Boss Caswell's Monkey's Saloon.* Ca. 1890. Patricia Bradbury Holton Collection, Salida Regional Library.

84 Logue, S.L. *Alpine Tunnel.* 1939. Salida Museum Negatives Collection, Salida Regional Library.

88 *Edison Electric Plant.* Salida Mail, January 1, 1903

93 *The Shavano Band.* Donna Nevens Collection, Salida Regional Library.

98 *Salida Granite Company.* Salida Museum Negatives Collection, Salida Regional Library.

99 *Salida Granite Company Shop.* Salida Museum Negatives Collection, Salida Regional Library.

100 *Mormon Battalion Monument.* Salida Museum Negatives Collection, Salida Regional Library.

104 *Cy Warman, Editor "Western Railway."* July 1890. The Railroad Trainmen's Journal, Vol. VII.

110 *Minstrel Band on Wagon.* Salida Centennial Collection, Salida Regional Library.

111 *Band in Salida.* Bob Rush Collection, Salida Regional Library.

112 *Henry Stroup's Application.* Salida Regional Library Collection.

117 *Young Men and Bicycles.* Salida Centennial Collection, Salida Regional Library.

123 *Coasting in the Rocky Mountains.* May 1883. The Wheelman, Vol. II, No. II.

128 *Hollis Spencer ca. 1891.* Hollis & Virginia Spencer Collection, Salida Regional Library.

135 *Duke.* Mountain Mail - Chaffee County Heritage edition, March 30, 1973.

136 *Monte Cristo Hotel.* Bob Rush Collection, Salida Regional Library.

140 *The D Street Suspension Bridge.* Salida Centennial Collection, Salida Regional Library.

145 *James Ramey.* Popular American Composers edited by Frank Boyden. New York: Herbert H. Taylor, 1902.

149 Hay, Henry. *Girls' Basketball Team.* The Tenderfoot, Salida High School, May 1910. Salida Regional Library Collection.

150 *Nina Churcher & Omer Divers at the Crater.* Salida Centennial Collection, Salida Regional Library.

152 *Hank, Bill, & Dusty.* Le Resume 1915, Salida High School, Salida Regional Library Collection.

155 *Ruth Hinshaw Spray.* Donna Nevens Collection, Salida Regional Library.

156 *Salida Library Postcard.* 1908. Salida Regional Library Collection.

157 *Library Cornerstone Laying.* May 1908. Jim Roll Collection, Salida Regional Library.

159 *Public Library, Salida, Colorado.* Ca. 1909. Anonymous Collection, Salida Regional Library.

162 *Red Cross at Library.* May 1918. Nancy Williams Collection, Salida Regional Library.

164 *Dr. George Hardin Curfman.* 1917. Charles S. Phalen Collection, Salida Regional Library.

168 *Ray Lines Funeral.* April 23, 1922. Bob Pierce Collection, Salida Regional Library.

169 *Ray Lines Funeral at Fairview Cemetery.* Bob Pierce Collection, Salida Regional Library.

171   Arens, Charles A. *Harry Bolton Crewdson.* Ca. 1915. Reprinted in Balloons to Jets: A Century of Aeronautics in Illinois, 1855-1955.

173   Pierce, Bob. *Crewdson Plane Wreck.* July 1919. Bob Pierce Collection, Salida Regional Library.

177   *The Ku Klux Klan on F Street.* Salida Museum Negatives Collection, Salida Regional Library.

180   *Frank Kelly.* Obituary, Salida Mail, August 18, 1950.

182   *Steam Shovel on Tenderfoot.* 1922. Bob Pierce Collection, Salida Regional Library.

186   *The First Big Air Show.* July 4, 1929. Salida Museum Collection, Salida, Colorado.

187   *Y&R Airways Plane at the Air Show.* July 4, 1929. Salida Museum Collection, Salida, Colorado.

190   *Hermit of Arbor Villa.* Hermit of Arbor Villa Collection, Salida Regional Library.

193   *Harold White.* Salida Mail, December 12, 1933.

195   *1933 Spartan Football Team.* Salida Centennial Collection, Salida Regional Library.

199   *1934 Spartan Football Team.* Salida Centennial Collection, Salida Regional Library.

202   *1935 Spartan Football Team.* Salida Centennial Collection, Salida Regional Library.

205   *Oliver's Stone.* Author's photograph.

211   Smith, Alta. *Frank Ashley and Thor Groswold.* Salida Record, February 15, 1938.

216   *Community Television Systems.* Salida Museum Negatives Collection, Salida Regional Library.

217 *Televents Community Television Systems.* Salida Museum Negatives Collection, Salida Regional Library.
218 *June Shaputis.* Obituary, Mountain Mail, October 28, 2019.
Back cover: *F Street from Spiral Drive, 2021.* Author's photograph. *Joy Skiing* by Damon Lange.

Index

295